To my real parents, Arthur and Edie Fripp,

and to my adopted parents,

Charlie "Tremendous" and Gloria Jones

CONTENTS

Introduction   1

Getting, Keeping, and Deserving Your Customers
    Develop an "unfair advantage"...   6
    Earn the right to do business...   8
    FRIPP TIP: People do business with...   11
    Treat every customer...   12
    FRIPP FABLE: "I love waking up with you..." 14
    Never overlook the opportunities...   15
    Don't take all the money...   19
    Ask what your customers want and expect...   21

Promote Yourself
    It doesn't matter how good you are...   26
    It's not your customer's job to remember you 28
    Make it obvious what you do   31
    FRIPP TIP: Promote yourself   33
    Introduce yourself provocatively   34
    Learn to schmooze   37
    Gain a reputation for doing the impossible   40
    Travel with your own PR agent   42
    FRIPP TIP: Build your booster section   45
    Ask nothing in return...   46
    FRIPP TIP: Learn from the best...and the worst! 48

MAKE IT

SO YOU DON'T HAVE TO FAKE IT

55 Fast-Acting Strategies
for Long-Lasting Success

Patricia Fripp

EB

Executive Books   **Mechanicsburg, PA**

By the author of *Get What You Want!*
and co-author of:
Insights into Excellence
Speaking Secrets of the Masters

Cover design by Dan Maddux and Donna Greenfield
Photo by Bob Adler
Editing by Eleanor Dugan
Proofreading by Patricia Lauterjung

Patricia Fripp
(800) 634-3035
e-mail PFripp@aol.com
http://www.fripp.com

Printed in the United States of America
Library of Congress Catalogue Card Number 99-65363
ISBN 0-937539-41-4
By
Executive Books
206 West Allen Street
Mechanicsburg, PA 17055
(800) 233-2665

www.executivebooks.com

First you impress, then you convince 49
Do something for nothing 51
FRIPP FABLE: Jay Leno 53
You can't please all the people... 54
The "secret" of success... 56
FRIPP TIP: Be employable, not just employed 58

Get in Touch, Keep in Touch

Technology does not run an enterprise 60
FRIPP TIP: Make sales meetings work for you 63
It's not who you know... 64
The real sale comes at the end of the sale 66
FRIPP FABLE: Customer service 68
Put on an event... 69
People learn more when they have fun 72
The currency of human contact... 74
The best of your best... 76
If you want to do business with the affluent 78
Use "Magic Words" 80
Express yourself with flair 83
Master technique 85
FRIPP TIP: Where do you want to be in five years? 89
Good marketing ends by asking... 90
FRIPP TIP: Five essentials of life... 92

Make Things Happen

If the world were perfect   94
Be limitless.   96
FRIPP TIP: Coping   99
What can be...   100
Resist emotional blackmail   102
Clean out the closets of your life   104
FRIPP TIP: Planning   106
Small additional increments   107
Learn to say "No"...   110
Gain two extra weeks a year...   113
Learn to be smarter...   116
FRIPP TIP: We are in charge...   118
Change your thinking just a few degrees...   119

Index   121

INTRODUCTION

I disagree with the popular adage, "Fake it till you make it." It reeks of "what if I get found out?" Making it means achieving happiness and success. Your definitions of "happiness" and "success" may be different from mine.

True happiness is having something to do where you can be totally you. For example, my job. I've always loved what I've done for a living, and I'm lucky that people have been eager to pay me to do it. Someone with an outgoing personality who wants a perfect excuse to meet interesting people is great for a sales career.

True success is doing for a living what you would do for nothing. If you suddenly had $10 million tomorrow, you wouldn't change your life very much. That's making it.

This book is dedicated to my parents, Arthur and Edie Fripp, and to what they taught me so I'd never have to fake it. Their actions and words—what I call Frippicisms—guided me to succeed and have kept me going strong ever since. Along the way, my brother Robert has contributed gems from his perceptive philosophy, and I've added many of my own Frippicisms which I'll share with you in this book.

Here are some Frippicisms from my family who helped me to think the way I do.

FRIPPICISM

Don't concentrate on making a lot of money. Concentrate on becoming the kind of person people want to do business with.

ARTHUR FRIPP

FRIPPICISM

In life, no one is dealt all the aces. You just have to play the hand you have better than other people.

ARTHUR FRIPP

FRIPPICISM

Discipline is not an end in itself, but a means to an end.

ROBERT FRIPP

FRIPPICISM

Yes, it's the inner you that counts, but you have to dress up and look good to attract people who can then find out how nice and interesting you are, and how valuable you can be to them.

EDIE FRIPP

FRIPPICISM

Style is being yourself, but on purpose. Act, think, dress, and feel like the person and success you want to be.

EDIE FRIPP

FRIPPICISM

Success is not who you know, but who wants to know you.

ARTHUR FRIPP

Tell me what you say you want. Then show me one week of your life, and I'll tell you if you'll get it.

When you decide you want to make it—the premise of this book—determine what you really want to do. Be sure that this is your own goal, not anyone else's, and that you have the motivation and commitment to reach it. Then make your efforts ongoing, consistent, relentless, sometimes shameless, and your way of life.

Once you've truly made it, your success belongs to you, your internal wealth is yours, and your pride in your achievements spills over into all areas of your personal and professional life. Learn how to make it so you never have to fake it.

Getting, Keeping, and Deserving

Your Customers

FRIPPICISM

Develop an "unfair advantage" over your competition.

All I've ever wanted in business is an *unfair advantage*. Before you raise your eyebrows, let me define the term. An unfair advantage is *not* lying, cheating, or stealing. It's exactly the opposite. An unfair advantage is doing everything just a little bit better than your competition. And even if you've been in business for many years and you're at the top of your profession, in today's competitive world you also need to do everything just a little bit better today than you did it yesterday. *That's* your unfair advantage.

It's not always easy. Do you remember the movie *Staying Alive*, the sequel to *Saturday Night Fever*? (And can you still dance that way?) It's about how the John Travolta character pursues a career as a professional dancer, all the highs and lows (with a little romance thrown in). The last scene is an incredible dance routine. As my friend Kookie and I danced out of the theater afterwards, I had a revelation: *The trouble with life is that it's just too short to be good at very many things!*

The dedication and discipline that the Travolta character needed to become a great dancer didn't leave him much time for anything else.

That's the problem with working and being in business today. The future belongs to those who are competent in *many different areas*. To be successful in any industry, you need to be a technically adept, charismatic communicator with exceptionally good work habits, good people skills, and an abundance of healthy energy (And it doesn't hurt if also you look good and dress well).

Start now to develop your own unfair advantage. What *one* thing can you do better than your competition? What *one* activity can you improve on?

FRIPPICISM

Earn the right to do business with people.

One successful young man I interviewed at a financial planners' meeting told me, "I used to be in another industry. I went into financial planning when I was thirty-three years old, joining my father's small firm. He'd been in the business for years, but I had to go out and get my own customers."

He drew up a list of twenty movers-and-shakers in his community, twenty affluent people with large spheres of influence who were eagerly pursued by everyone in the investment community. This young man had very little experience. He hadn't yet "earned their business."

He called on each of these people and said, "I am new to this business. I know you know about my father, but you don't know me. I am not trying to sell you. I know I haven't earned the right yet. However, could I please have a ten-minute interview? Would you, as a leader in the community, tell me what I should do to earn the right to do business with people like you?"

See what he did? He made it safe. He told them up front that he wasn't going to try to sell them anything. He only wanted ten minutes.

Frankly, I think you have to be very lucky to get ten minutes of an important person's time. But he presented it in such an appealing way that no one turned him down. And he kept his side of the bargain. After ten minutes, he left unless they invited him to stay longer.

At the end of his first year, three of those people actually gave him a small portion of their portfolio to manage to see how he would do. At the end of three years, seven out of the original twenty people had placed a portion of their investments with his firm. He'd earned the right.

I used to say that there are two kinds of people to market to: those who know and love us and those who never heard of us. You can advertise traditionally and on the Internet, network and join organizations, send out direct mail, and do a combination of activities to get new business. But please don't think these methods substitute for keeping in touch with the people who now know you and love you. These are people who've inquired, whom you've met at a meeting, who've done some business with you in the past. Keep in touch with these valuable resources!

When Homer Dunn was an up-and-coming salesperson at IBM, he told me there are actually *three* kinds of people that he calls on. "First, there are the people I've already made a sale to." (This was in the mainframe days, so it was a big sale.) "I keep calling on these customers, making sure they are satisfied with the product and the service." That's maintaining a sale.

"Then there are the people I'm calling on, those who are in the sales cycle, which can be a long-term process." (And, with really high-ticket items, this can be a really long-term process!)

"Finally, there are the people I want to do business with. I have not earned the right yet to do business with these people, but I am maintaining a relationship, letting them know of my progress and success. So when I have finally earned the right to the sale, they are all mine."

What are you doing now to earn the right to people's business? Who in your community have you targeted?

FRIPP TIP

There's an old saying, "If you build a better mousetrap, people will beat a path to your door." That was true once, but not today. Having the best product or service does not automatically guarantee you success. That's because:

1. People do business with people they know.

2. People do business with the people who do business with them.

3. People do business with people their friends talk about.

4. People do business with people they read about.

FRIPPICISM

Treat all your customers as if they are the only one in the world.

My first boss treated every customer magnificently. It was a terrific lesson in customer service. They could be rich or humble, young or old, a resident of the hotel penthouse suite or a waitress in the hotel coffee shop. Each one got the same star treatment.

Now that I have a greater understanding of business, I recognize how truly smart he was. I've learned that a waitress with fairly affluent customers can have a far greater sphere of influence than a society lady who only plays bridge or lunches with some friends a few times a week. The waitress talks to several hundred people a day. You'll do business with many people who won't become your biggest customers, but whose *spheres of influence* can be worth more to you than those of your larger accounts.

One of my friends, Gary Richter, is the President of the First National Bank of Naples, an outrageously successful "boutique" bank in Naples, Florida. Late one Friday afternoon, an elderly woman called and said she needed to cash a $200 check. The bank closed in ten minutes, and she was twenty minutes away. Many of us would say, "Of course, please come over, we'll stay open for you." But Gary's bank believes in giving exceptional service. One of their employees brought her $200 cash on his way home and picked up her endorsed check.

As it turned out, the woman had her extensive financial holdings at a large national bank. After her positive experience, she asked if they could handle all her financial needs. "Yes," said Gary. So she moved all her assets and investments to Gary's bank.

"I tell my employees," says Gary, "that if we roll out the red carpet for a billionaire, they won't even notice. If we roll it out for millionaires, they expect it. If we roll out the red carpet for thousandaires, they appreciate it. And if we roll out the red carpet for hundredaires, they tell everybody they know!" You can literally take that advice to the bank. Six years after the bank opened, it grew from 16 employees to 180, and from $6 million to $330 million.

Obviously, we all want the big accounts. Unless you're huge like Starbucks, you can't make a living dealing exclusively with small orders. But always think long-term and big-picture. Small-order customers who are active and visible in their fields, in their professional associations, or in their communities are great customers because of the people they know and the people they tell.

Treat all your customers magnificently, and you can't fail. What have you done recently to show your customers they are invaluable to you? Have you developed the "Roll out the red carpet" attitude?

FRIPP FABLE

One of my hairstyling clients, Hank Torchiani, used to come in at 7:45 in the morning once a month for the last eight years that I had my salon. One day I dropped him this note: "Hank, have I told you recently how much I love waking up with you once a month?" (Naturally I sent that to his office, not his home. I'm not a troublemaker!)

The next time he came in he said, "Patricia, that was such a nice note, I'm keeping it in my box of treasures." He died in 1987, and I am very grateful I had communicated how much I enjoyed not only his patronage but also his friendship.

FRIPPICISM

Never overlook the opportunities right under your nose.

A re you overlooking customers in your backyard? When you want publicity and promotion, you've got to come up with a unique idea. It's nice to be able to say, "The Chamber of Commerce thinks we have an interesting business," but my friend Jonathan Stone came up with a more dynamic promotional idea for his enterprise. His claim was, "The bike messengers think we have the coolest office in San Francisco!"

Do you know what bike messengers are? If your community doesn't have a dense downtown district, you might not have seen them. In San Francisco, a whole subculture of bike messengers races from one high-rise office building to another. These young men and women are often pierced and tattooed, their hair in colors God never thought of for the rainbow. They work for minimum wage under enormous pressure in all kinds of weather, and they love their jobs because they have so much power. They can zip down the street and make gentlemen in Brioni suits scatter. They are on a combat mission to deliver an important packet.

Jonathan Stone's firm, Another Dancing Bear Productions, sells promotional advertising pieces. Always bubbling with creative ideas, Jonathan phoned The Business Times and said, "I've got a great idea for you. Why not do an article profiling 'The Ten Coolest Offices in San Francisco According to the Bike Messengers'? And, by the way, my office is one of them!" But The Business Times wasn't interested.

Have you ever had a brilliant idea but couldn't sell it? Jonathan was really frustrated. I said, "Jonathan, don't worry. I'll think about it and come up with something." The next time I was near his office, I decided to drop in to see it.

First, a cute young man stepped into the elevator behind me. "Can I press your button for you?" I asked. "Nine," he replied (Forget what your mother told you -- *Always* talk to strangers! Remember: People do business with people they know; people do business with people who do business with them; people do business with people their friends talk about; and people do business, sometimes, with people they talk to in elevators).

I asked the young man, "Do you work in this building or are you visiting?" "I work for So-and-So on the ninth floor," he said. What about you?" I told him I was visiting my friend Jonathan Stone at Another Dancing Bear Productions, tenth floor. "I hear he has a really cool office," I said. "Have you been there?" "No," he said, "never heard of them."

When I got to the tenth floor, I discovered that Jonathan hadn't exaggerated. You don't actually open a door into his private office. You step through a bear-shaped cutout that looks as if a bear had bashed through the door. On the opposite wall, you see the back of the bear, as if it collided with the brick wall. The reception area walls are covered with all the bright, colorful, and inventive products that specialty advertisers sell. I can see why the bike kids think it is cool.

"Do I have an idea for *you!*" I told Jonathan. "Do you realize, you could quadruple your business without even leaving the building? I just met a young man who works in this building and has never heard of you. This is an enormous building. You should do an *event*. Invite everyone in the building," I told him, "but one floor at a time. You couldn't handle the traffic if everyone showed up." Send out a really colorful flyer that says something like:

Come see the Coolest Office in San Francisco, according to the Bike Messengers!
Right here in this building
Friday, 5:00 to 7:00 P.M.

Free hors d'oeuvres and a free doodad for every visitor.

SPECIAL DRAWING
Enter a drawing to win $200 off your first
or next order of advertising specialties or premiums.

Your best potential customers may be right under your nose. When I was in the hairstyling business, I remember calling on a hairstylist named Rod who had an absolutely spectacular salon in a brand new shopping center. But the shopping center hadn't taken off, and neither had his business.

He told me defensively, "I have customers who drive all the way from Fresno so I can cut their hair."

"Rod," I said, "get a life! People who drive eighty miles for a haircut feed your ego. What feeds your family is the people who live or work in a five-minute radius. I'm not saying that you can't rent a bus to bring your customers and their friends from Fresno, but concentrate your flyers and your walking around shaking hands closer to home."

What about all those people in your office or apartment building, in your shopping center, in your Chamber of Commerce, gym, PTA, church, street, and all your different spheres of influence close to home? Does every one of these people know who you are and what you do and why you're so good at it? Can you come up with a good way to tell them?

FRIPPICISM

Don't take all the money that's on the table.

Do you have any "friends" who call only when they want something? Are they your favorite people? Do you contact customers only when you're asking for their money? Or do you keep in touch for other reasons? Do salespeople call on you only when they want you to spend money? What if, instead, they called you with a lead, a referral, or an idea? Wouldn't that make you think you were more than just a customer? That they cared about you and your business?

In yesterday's world, we celebrated closing a sale. Today, we celebrate opening a relationship. That's how a business is built. One of the goals in growing your business should be that the same person you sold to today will still be spending money with you ten years from now. People want to do business with people who appreciate them and look out for their interests. Be appropriately generous with your ideas and time.

If you want to be perceived as an irreplaceable unpaid advisor by your customers, phone them now and then, saying something like, "Hey, I've got an idea that might work for you." Or, "I've got a potential customer for you" or "Here's something that might help your business." Absolutely no strings and no expectation of an order.

It pays not to take all the money on the table. Always give your customers more than they pay for. What can you do to make yourself an unpaid advisor so you become invaluable to your customers and guarantee their loyalty?

FRIPPICISM
Ask what your customers want and expect before your competitors do.

S atisfy your customers...or someone else will. Your prospects and customers can give you important feedback, both directly and indirectly. After addressing a group of sales contest winners in Hawaii, I was on the shuttle bus headed for the airport. My usual custom is to ask questions, so I said to the driver, "I bet your passengers tell you what they really think about their stays at these fancy resorts because they know you don't work for any of them."

"Oh, yes," he replied. "In fact, once a month, the general manager of the hotel where you stayed comes to the depot with a big box of donuts and has coffee with the drivers. While we eat his donuts, we tell him everything we've overheard about his hotel -- and about his competitors' hotels."

That is what I call Box-of-Donuts consulting. The hotel manager could have paid large fees to a research firm that would phone 1,000 guests and ask what they liked and didn't like. But that information couldn't possibly be as up-to-date or as honest as these drivers' feedback, nor would it give him valuable information about his competition.

Do you get, keep, and deserve your customers by finding out what they really want from you? The most frequently overlooked low-tech method is to talk to someone who talks to your customers and has no vested interest in their opinions. But this doesn't mean you don't also interview them formally.

The Ritz-Carlton Hotels, famous for customer service, do regular formal surveys with cards in the rooms and mailings. Someone asked their president, Horst Schulze, "Why don't you offer a 'frequent guest' program?" (Such programs are a major investment of organizational time and philosophical strategy). Schulze replied, "We don't because only two percent of our customers have asked for them. What our customers *do* want is to have a bowl of fresh fruit in the room when they check in." So that's what the Ritz-Carlton Hotels provide. When you know what people really want, it is rarely difficult or expensive to make them feel special. Schulze was doing exactly right.

My friend David Garfinkel, author of *The Money-Making Copywriting Course*, says there are five important answers you need to get from your customers, directly or indirectly:

1. What do you like about buying from us?
2. Why did you buy from us in the first place?
3. What problems did you have before you
   bought from us?
4. How did we help you solve those problems?
5. How are things better for you now?

"That last answer," says David, "is very important. It's what a positive result looks like to a real customer, and it's going to look the same to your other customers and prospects when you tell them about it."

Start some creative brainstorming. Consider who else might know what your customers are thinking. Is there some comfortable and ethical way you can talk with these people? One-on-one questioning? Maybe invite a group for a breakfast? Think about who in your business knows what your customers want. Is there a service that can provide you with an effective, economical market sample?

Finding out what your customers want may seem obvious, but too often it's overlooked. After my morning program for a Fortune 100 company, I found the attendees were spending the afternoon seated at round tables, brainstorming the topic, "How can we give our customers better service?" Very innocently, I asked my client, "Oh, and where are the customers you've invited to sit in with your salespeople?" There weren't any. (This was like doing a survey of what hospital patients want by asking the doctors).

One way to maintain your "unfair advantage" in business is to research your competition so you know what they're offering, then research your prospects' wants and needs so you can do more for them as customers than your competition. For example, a Federal Express executive, Gurn Freeman, told me how, early in his career, he decided he wanted to go into the moving business. First, he opened the Yellow Pages and saw 128 movers listed. He phoned the first twenty-five and made an appointment for someone to come and talk to him, saying he was moving to Phoenix. At the end of every interview, he took notes on what they had done right, how they could have done better, and anything they did wrong. Next, he put together his own sales strategy.

Gurn quickly became a top mover's representative. "My secret was to do something none of those other reps had done for me. If I had an appointment with someone who was moving to Phoenix, I would call the Phoenix Chamber of Commerce and get all their free information and brochures for my prospective customer. I made it obvious that I had done my research before the sales appointment so I deserved their business. And I nearly always got it."

Of course, you will come up with great ideas for serving your customers, but there is nothing like asking them what they need, want, and appreciate. (The Ritz-Carlton Hotels changed the style of their room locks three times in eleven years to address the changing preferences and security concerns of their guests). Asking shows your customers how important they are to you. It's how you satisfy them and keep them from going elsewhere.

Why should you try so hard to find out what your customers really want? Because your best customers are also the hottest prospects for your competitors. Satisfy them before someone else does! If other salespeople win over one of your loyal customers by offering more ideas and more service, maybe they have more right to the business than you do.

If you're not quite sure, isn't it a good idea to go to your customers and say, "Tell me, in your own words, what I have done for you?"

When you lose a customer, you lose two ways:

1.   You don't get their money.

2.   Your competitors do.

What are you doing right now to deserve your customers' business?

Promote Yourself

FRIPPICISM

It doesn't matter how good you are. The world has to know it.

My friend Alan Weiss says, "If you don't toot your own horn, there is no music." As you market yourself, your self-promotion must be ongoing, consistent, relentless, and sometimes *shameless*. I'm shameless when I hand out buttons at my speeches that say, "I've been FRIPPnotized." I tell my audiences, "I want you to remember me, but much more important, I want you to remember what FRIPP stands for: Frequently Reinforce Ideas that are Productive and Profitable."

Shameless self-promotion is part of my nature, but most people resort to it only when they've hit a stone wall with a prospect and have nothing to lose. My friend Tom Carson turned a charming but shameless act into a long-term business relationship. He sold medical equipment and had called on one hospital for four years without a nibble. One day he decided he'd give up after one last try. In the hospital lobby, he saw a sign, "Flowers 50% off." He bought the largest bouquet they had, attached a note, and delivered them to the buyer without saying a word. The card read, "This is a shameless attempt to curry favor with Marilyn, the very influential buyer. Best wishes, Tom Carson." She laughed and pinned the card to a nearby bulletin board where it stayed for five years.

That year, she converted every piece of business she could to his company, earning Tom Carson and his wife a bonus trip to the Virgin Islands. Marilyn is now long retired and Tom has moved on, but his old company is still selling to the hospital. Because of Tom's one shameless action, his company is still benefiting two decades later.

If, like me, you sell a service that people use occasionally rather than frequently, you need to be as memorable as possible so they will remember and buy from you again. Keep shameless self-promotion in your arsenal. Be sure you are comfortable with yourself, and always attach it to a smile. If you do, it will serve you well.

What prospects have you almost given up on that are ready for the shameless, jump-start treatment?

FRIPPICISM

It is not your customers' job to remember you. It's your job to make sure they don't have the opportunity to forget you.

A re you fabulous at what you do? If you think you're not getting the recognition you deserve, you have to take charge of making it happen.

There is no point going anywhere if people won't remember you were there. A key part of your self-advertising marketing strategy is to be noticed. Happily, this does not mean you have to arrive on a skateboard or be loud and boisterous.

At the National Speakers Association and in San Francisco, I am well known for my hats. I happen to love them. They are also part of my overall marketing strategy to be noticed. Often at large events, I'm the only one with a hat, which sparks people to start a conversation: "Oh, I like your hat. My mother used to wear hats." And, I say, "Yes, they make nice people like you talk to me. Hello, I'm Patricia. Who are you?" People talk to me who would never initiate conversation with others. That's part of what gives me an "unfair advantage."

Men rarely wear hats indoors, but I met a young man at a gathering in Denver who'd devised a great attention-getter of his own. When I was talking to him, I noticed his lapel pin was upside down. I automatically turned it around, and he smiled. "I always wear it that way so people like you reach out and fix it." The fact that I touched him gave him his "unfair advantage."

See what I mean? Your "unfair advantage" is connecting with and engaging potential business contacts by doing many simple things like this on an ongoing, consistent, relentless basis. Just do things a little bit better, more creatively, or more innovatively than your competition does.

One woman who sold a new cookware line had a booth at an industry event. Because her cookware was not well known and people kept walking past her display, she decided to do a "Frippy." That evening she ran out and bought a handsome hat. During the rest of the trade show, as people passed, they'd say, "I like your hat." She'd reply, "You like my hat? You should see my cookware! Come in." Three years later, she had built her business from nothing to $18 million. She had made it easy for people to talk to her. From the conversation came relationships. It works.

Be sure to greet everyone at networking events. Don't ignore people you recognize just because you've forgotten their names. Smile and ask a provocative question like "What is the most exciting thing that's happened to you since we met?" "What is your greatest recent success?" or "What are you most looking forward to?" And never feel afraid to say, "The last time we met, we had such a great conversation. Remind me what your name is?" My friend Susan RoAne tells people, "Forgive me for forgetting your name. Since I passed forty, it's hard to remember my own."

As follow-up, always send a note or brochure the next day to the people you have met. Keep their cards, and make notes of what you said for the next time you meet them at another event.

These are all positive, pleasant, easy ways to be memorable. Get the most out of your networking time and energy by making yourself worth remembering!

For many years, Max Gunther, author of *The Luck Factor*, has studied what makes someone "lucky." "These people make themselves known to many other people," he says, "usually without thinking about it. They're gregarious. They go out of their way to be friendly. They talk to strangers. They're joyous meeters and greeters. If they sit next to someone on an airplane, they start a conversation. The guy who sells them their morning newspaper is more than just a face." People such as this increase the odds of being noticed and remembered favorably.

Make yourself noticed in your community. Join professional associations and networking groups, then participate. Volunteer to co-chair a committee or work on a special project. If you're shy, agree to serve as a greeter at local charity or Chamber of Commerce meetings. It'll be a great opportunity to meet new prospects and have them introduced to you.

You are the Chairman of the Board of your own career! No one else is going to care about your future the way you do. Do you have an ongoing, consistent, relentless strategy to be known to your prospects and customers? In your community? In your industry? How are you making yourself memorable?

Remember:

- "Hello" can lead to a conversation.
- A conversation can lead to a relationship.
- A relationship can lead to profitable business.

FRIPPICISM

Make it obvious what you do.

My friend Marla recently inherited some money and decided to buy her first house. She quickly discovered that Realtors are like parking spots. When you don't need one, you run into them all the time, but once you want one, you're not sure where to start looking.

Now, imagine that Marla had gone to her aerobics class and suddenly noticed the person in front of her had a tee shirt with an advertising logo for a major Realtor. I'm not saying this gets them her business, but it is sure to start a conversation, and every conversation has the potential for starting a relationship. Every relationship has the potential for leading to business. And if you nurture those business relationships, they have the potential for long-time profit. There might be four Realtors in that class, but the one with the tee shirt will start the conversation.

I challenge you to make it really obvious what you do. There are many ways. One is to introduce yourself in a memorable way. Another is silent advertising. Let's say that you have an XYZ franchise or represent a company or product. Are all your kids walking around in XYZ tee shirts? Are you, in your designer outfit, at least carrying your papers in an XYZ bag? When I addressed the Subway Sandwich franchise owners, I challenged them. "You made a major investment in your franchise," I told them, "but I am the only person in this room wearing a Subway Sandwich lapel pin. The only person wearing a Subway Sandwich watch. The only person here who walked in with my materials in a Subway Sandwich tote bag. Never overlook opportunities of wearing your advertising."

People can read about you and your company in the newspaper and Yellow Pages, but they also read the logo on your shirt or tote bag when you're at the gym, on the commuter bus or train, shopping or jogging, or walking down the street. (My own tee shirts say "Frequently Reinforce Ideas that are Productive and Profitable" on the front, an acronym for Fripp, while my various Frippicism slogans are on the back.)

Can people tell what you do by looking at you? How are you advertising yourself and your business in a way that encourages questions, conversations, and the beginning of a business relationship?

FRIPP TIP

You handle mountains of details and a crisis or two every day for your organization, but how much of your expertise and energy do you put into promoting *yourself*? I've worked closely with everyone from top executives to managers and salespeople for more than two decades, and I'm amazed at how many don't have an overall marketing strategy for their own careers.

It's not hard. You already possess the skills. Just put as much commitment and planning into selling yourself as you do into your organization. Modesty may be a virtue, but it's hardly vanity to make others aware of your achievements.

FRIPPICISM

Introduce yourself provocatively.

Every time you meet someone new, you have the perfect opportunity for an unforgettable info-mercial. Yet most people make a pitiful job of it.

Have you ever asked someone what they did and had them give you some high-falutin' title so you were still in the dark? If you don't know what someone does, how could you ever decide if you want to do business with them? And why should you remember them?

To make the most of your Seven Super Seconds the next time you introduce yourself, develop an intriguing "tag line" to follow your name. Say something about yourself that will grab attention, make people want to ask you questions, and stick in their minds later. When asked what I do, I like to say, "I make conventions and sales meetings more exciting."

My friend Susan RoAne asked a customer at her favorite coffee shop, "I see you here all the time. What do you do?" He replied with an irresistible and humorous tag line, "I help rich people sleep at night." Susan laughed. "You must be either a pharmacist or a financial planner," she said. He admitted to the latter. Now, whenever she runs into him, she can greet him by name and ask, "How are those rich people sleeping these days?" He has made himself and his profession memorable.

An excellent way to get people to remember you is by belonging to business and civic organizations. Get out, be involved, make yourself known. One I belong to is a group of dynamic businesswomen called the Continental Breakfast Club (CBC). Like most such organizations, everyone stands at each gathering and states their name and company.

This is your golden opportunity. Wait until the applause or the laughter for the previous person has finished. Then project your voice so everyone can hear, state your name, and use your memorable tag line.

Sheryl Krajewski, a long-time CBC member, has developed such a memorable introduction routine that she doesn't even have to give it. Her business is Hats on Post, and she always wears striking hats. (I'm one of her best customers.) Sheryl stands and says, "Sheryl Krajewski," and pauses expectantly. The entire group responds in unison, "Hats on Post!"

Another tag line I've never forgotten was that of Fred O. Foster at the Executives Association (Their slogan is "Remember a Member First"). Fred always introduced himself as "Fred O. Foster Wines & Spirits," running his name and company name together. I haven't belonged to that club since 1984, but whenever I run into Fred O. Foster, it is impossible not to greet him, "Hi, Fred O. Foster Wines & Spirits." For many years, whenever I needed a thank-you present, his name sprang to my lips, and I found myself telling my assistant, "Call Fred O. Foster Wines & Spirits."

The Business Times ran a story about Jonathan Stone who introduces himself by quoting his business card. First his name, then the name of his company, and finally his advertising tag line: "Hi, I'm Jonathan Stone, Another Dancing Bear Productions–We Put Your Name on Stuff." This is simple and brilliant.

His introduction so impressed me that I began citing it as a good example in my presentations. After one of them, a man came up and introduced himself: "Hi, I'm Jonathan Stone, Another Dancing Bear Productions–We Put Your Name on Stuff. Thanks for the plug!" We have since become friends.

Business networking gatherings are great opportunities for introducing yourself in a memorable way, but they can be pretty daunting if you don't know anyone. Here are some strategies.

First, whenever someone asks what you do, don't answer with just a job title or a company. Give your information in such an intriguing way that 99.9 percent of your listeners will respond with a question like, "How do you do that?" Their question then ends up being an invitation for you to give a mini sales presentation.

Here's what I do. I walk in wearing a terrific hat (a great conversation starter) and head for the cheese dip. If you have a hard time connecting with strangers in groups, go where the food is. A buffet lends itself to ice breakers like, "Doesn't that look good? Oh, have you ever seen tomatoes that red? Tell me, do you know what that is?" Unless the other person is incredibly shy, you've started an exchange.

Then you get in a conversation, "Hi, I'm Patricia." "Hi, I'm Jeannie." "What do you do, Jeannie?" "I'm in the hotel business. And what do *you* do?"

"I make conventions and sales meetings more exciting," I tell them. Almost invariably, my new friend has to ask, "How do you do that?" Immediately, I get to market myself: "You know how companies have meetings that are supposed to be stimulating, and they're often dull and boring? Well, I have some practical ideas I present in an entertaining way. The result is people stay awake, have a good time, and get the company's message. My name is Patricia Fripp. I'm a professional speaker."

Then I get to ask them, "What do you do in the hotel business?" They tell me, and, if they also use a catchy tag line, I can say, "Wow, that sounds interesting. Tell me about it." We have connected in a memorable way.

FRIPPICISM

Learn to schmooze— or lose.

---

chmoozing (connecting positively in a social situation)
increases your "like factor," and your "like factor" can give
you the edge over others who are more experienced. All
other things being equal–same price, same merchandise, same
business opportunity–the like factor will get you the business
every time.

One morning I was dressed up to give a speech for the IRS.
(They've gotten so much of my money that I wanted to get some
of theirs.) Afterward, I arrived for an appointment with a
potential client in downtown San Francisco. His secretary said he
would be a half-hour late and offered me a cup of coffee.
However, I decided to use the thirty minutes to buy a pair of
pantyhose at a nearby store.

As I walked in, this dynamic, incredible, fun sales assistant
greeted me. She said, "Good afternoon. Don't you look nice?
How can I help you?" She took initiative and wasn't helping
anyone.

"Oh, I just need a pair of pantyhose," I said. After I'd bought
the hose, she commented, "How about some terrific new shoes
to go with them?"

"I'll be honest," I said. "I have so many shoes that Imelda Marcos stops by to admire them. But I have twenty-five minutes. I'll look." I let her show me shoes, and she was a lot of fun. You know how, when people are fun to do business with, you sometimes end up spending more money than you planned to? Well, there I was, admiring my new turquoise shoes.

"You really do look nice," she said. "What do you do?" I told her that I traveled worldwide talking about good and bad customer service.

"I could tell by the way you were dressed you were somebody important," she said.

With sixteen more minutes to go, I decided to tell her how important. "Next week I'm attending the convention of the National Speakers Association. They are going to make me their first female president."

"For somebody *that* important," she said, "do I have a dress for you!" I had gone in to kill twenty-eight minutes and buy some pantyhose. I ended up with two pairs of hose, turquoise shoes, and an exorbitantly expensive beaded evening dress. Until I met this clever young woman, I had no idea I was important enough to deserve such an expensive dress.

This saleswoman was absolutely shameless–and she'd never even heard me speak. She knew, just as you should know, that exceptionally good customer service plus the "like factor" are exceptionally good for sales.

Let's analyze what she did right. First of all, she had what I call the "schmooze factor." She was perfectly appropriate and professional, but she schmoozed. She made sure I had a good time, that we had a pleasant interaction. It was so nice talking to her that I was in no hurry to leave.

The next thing she did was something she didn't do. She didn't take me at my word when I told her clearly that I wasn't there to spend money. (Probably she decided I looked like someone who carries credit cards). She kept offering suggestions, no high pressure, but in a fun and entertaining way.

Look, I'm a sales trainer–I knew exactly what she was doing, and I loved every second of it. It was her job, and she did it so well that it almost became my job to find something else I could buy from her. We had bonded, and I felt obligated. What a great salesperson.

Another day, I went to my neighborhood electronics store to buy a pack of batteries. I was wearing jeans and a cap, no make up. I thought, "If they do everything that I suggest in my seminars, if they schmooze, if they are observant, if they don't prejudge me for not being all dressed up, if they keep asking, and if they deserve my business, I might just spend more."

And that particular day they did everything right. They didn't prejudge, they were observant, they made comments, they schmoozed, they were friendly, they made good human contact, and they made it fun to interact. Besides my batteries, I bought a mobile phone, another tape recorder, and a television/VCR combo—all things that I planned to buy eventually, but not that specific day.

Do you make it fun to do business with you? Cultivate your likability and schmooze techniques—not overly personal or intrusive, but bright, interested, and professional. You'll stand out from your competition every time—and your customers will probably tell their friends.

> ## FRIPPICISM
>
> *Gain a reputation for doing the impossible.*

You're invaluable in the marketplace when you build a reputation for doing the impossible. It makes you indispensable.

Before you insist you can't do the impossible, let me explain. "Doing the impossible" simply means taking on jobs other people think they can't do and achieving positive results, using creativity and innovation. When others put limits on what can be expected of them, you stand out by achieving what they have refused to try.

My friend Judi Moreo is a good example. She had her own special events and convention business in Las Vegas. No request was impossible. For example, when the Desert Inn opened a new wing, it took Judi less than a week to locate 126 women who looked alike and dress them identically so they could line the entrance to greet guests. (Desert Inn General Manager Burton Cohen said, "If you want the possible done, call anyone. If you want the impossible, call Judi Moreo.")

Do you understand what an "unfair advantage" you have if your customers think you can do the impossible? People never ask you how much you charge.

If you're *still* sitting there thinking "Yes, but I can't *do* the impossible!" then you don't understand what the impossible really is. Look for creative ways to add value for your customers that other sales people can't or don't do. The *impossible* is anything that you can do but other people think they can't do. For me, the impossible is trying to remember how to work complex office equipment and shipping forms while my assistant is on vacation. There was a time that I thought running a computer was impossible, until I learned how to do it.

Most people are too modest. When you can do something–anything–that others regard as impossible, you've made yourself indispensable. Just let everyone know about it in a nice way.

What can you or could you do better than anyone else?

FRIPPICISM

Travel with your own PR agent.

For that extra edge at networking events, here's a very inexpensive technique I'll bet you never heard before: Travel with your own public relations representative. In other words, go with a partner.

Enlist a coworker, friend, or relative to form a duo. My networking buddy in San Francisco is Susan RoAne, the best-selling author of *How to Work a Room, Secrets of Savvy Networking*, and *What Do I Say Next?* We attend many meetings together.

Here's what we do. When we arrive at an event, we alternately separate and come together. I'll walk up to Susan as she is talking to someone, and she'll say, "Laura, let me introduce you to Patricia Fripp. Patricia is truly one of the greatest speakers in the country." And, I will turn around and say, "Laura, I bet Susan is too modest to tell you she's the best-selling author of three books."

When you do this, you're saying great things about each other that you'd love your prospects to know, but modesty prevents you from telling them.

Suppose Natalie and Fred are secret partners. As Fred walks up, Natalie says to the person she's been talking to, "Jack, I'd like you to meet Fred. Fred has taught me nearly everything I know about sales and our product line. There has never been a sales contest in our company he hasn't won." Then, Fred can say, "Well, Natalie's being very generous. It's true, I've been with our company for sixteen years. But, Natalie's been here for only six months, and she's brought in more new business than any other person in the fifty-three year history of our firm, so she knows a couple of things too. Much as I'd love to help you, I tell you, you couldn't do better than work with someone as enthusiastic as Natalie."

That's what I call "traveling with your own PR agent." Would this technique work for you? Who would be a good PR partner for your next networking event?

Here's another way to acquire a roving battalion of PR agents. My friend Cheryl Austin Brown left her business in Toronto and relocated to Scottsdale, Arizona with her husband. Her extensive labor practice had included negotiating collective agreements, mediating management-labor disputes, arguing arbitration cases, and doing management training. Happily, many of her former colleagues and employers were able to give her business there or recommend her to others, but it was tougher than she thought to replicate her old business. But she figured out a way that worked.

For the first four months, she attended up to seventeen meetings a week to learn how business was done in that part of the world and to meet people she could learn from and who could hire her. She volunteered for professional associations that fit areas of her expertise. During this time, many of the projects she was offered were outside her experience. Instead of grabbing them, figuring anything is better than nothing, she referred these projects to people she had met who were fully qualified. These people respected her decision and valued her recommendation, so they became walking PR for her integrity and focus. It was tough with no income coming in, but it would have been tougher to fail. Cheryl knew she was creating a reputation with every decision. Finally, after five months, she signed three training and consulting contracts. One gave her three years of work. Her patience and PR reps had paid off.

Who among your customers and friends can you consider your unofficial PR agents?

FRIPP TIP

Build Your Booster Section.

You add to your value by having a group of people who are on your side. Keep in touch with colleagues. Send frequent and unforgettable notes or e-mails to your professional friends. Congratulate them whenever they're promoted or recognized for some achievement, or just write to say how much you enjoy working with them.

Professional associations are great sources of boosters. As a member, you continue your education while meeting your industry leaders and trendsetters. When you volunteer to chair a committee or work on a special project, you make others aware of your commitment to your industry.

> ## FRIPPICISM
>
> *To be really memorable, give something of value and ask nothing in return.*

As preparation for a presentation, I interviewed a group of school photographers who were the most successful in their profession. Then, I encouraged everyone in the audience to seek out these people to study and learn from them.

One of the most successful men in the industry told me, "When I worked in a camera store, one of our suppliers really impressed me. He always tucked a little something extra in his shipments. It might have only been some Tootsie Rolls, but always something.

"I made up my mind that, when I went into business for myself, I would budget ten percent of the gross for promotions, and these promotions wouldn't be expensive ads or displays. Instead, I'd give small gifts to people." In the very beginning, he actually put ten cents of each incoming dollar in an old coffee can.

The more money he made, the more he gave away, restricting himself to high-caliber gifts with his name on them. He also reasoned that people place orders when they are in a work environment so he focused on "something they are going to keep on their desk or in their office rather than something they are going to take home." One of his student giveaways was a ruler with all the Presidents plus his contact information. Teachers would routinely call him, asking for more rulers: "We're doing a lesson about the American Presidents this week."

One of the something-for-nothing gifts I give my clients is a break on postage when they order from overseas. I sell a lot of books, audio tapes, and video tapes to Hong Kong and Australia via the Internet, and airfreight costs can be high. If, for example, the cost is $60, I absorb $20 and charge $40, but I also give the customer more than $40 worth of free merchandise. No one is penalized for ordering from half way around the world.

I also give some of my clients heart-shaped bookmarks that say, "You don't close a sale; you open a relationship." Consider creating your own heart-related promotional item that says, "We've opened our heart to you" or "You're more than just a customer." If you ship products in boxes, why not enclose small inexpensive gift items, something as simple as a handful of wrapped candy or a useful advertising specialty with your name on it? Whatever you do, your message should be, "You're not just money to us. We like you and have a relationship with you."

Sometimes giving something away brings you more returns in the long run than if you charged for it. What can you give your customers without looking like you're asking for something in return?

FRIPP TIP

Learn from the best...and the worst!

Here's a homework assignment. No matter how long you've been in the work force, make a list of every boss you've had. Start with your first job at the age of ten or twelve and go right through to today. What did you learn from each of these people, good or bad?

This exercise is especially important if you are now in management or plan to be. Everyone you've ever worked for can teach you something, even if it is only to provide you with a pitiful example of what *not* to do.

"If you want to build a ship," wrote pilot-poet Antoine de Saint-Exupery, "don't drum up people together to collect wood and don't assign them tasks and work, but rather teach them to long for the endless immensity of the sea." How many leaders have gone beyond mere management to filling you with a yearning for the endless immensity of opportunities before you? How did they do it?

FRIPPICISM

First you impress. Then you convince.

If your marketing impresses your prospects and customers, is that good enough? No. It has to convince them too. Copywriting genius David Garfinkel constantly reminds me of this. The difference between impressing and convincing is the difference between awards and rewards. People can go "Oooh, aaah," and think something looks really wonderful, and that's like getting an award. But they haven't reached for their wallet to reward you with their business. You still have to convince them.

People don't buy just because they're dazzled or blown away by what they see. They buy because they're also convinced you can do the job, you will deliver the value and quality, your track record is solid, and you'll be around five years from now if they need you.

Here are four ways your marketing can convince them.

1. By the obvious quality of your information. Many marketers send out "free information," "valuable information," even "money-making information," at no charge as a small sample of what you'll get when you actually pay money.

2. By the clarity of your information, how easily they can understand what you're saying. People don't buy when they're confused. One of my clients asked my opinion of his newest sales letter. "I don't even know what it says," I told him honestly.

"First, the print is too small. I have to put on glasses to read it. Then, the over-all faded look is supposed to be very sophisticated, but again that means I can't read it. And there's not a single bold statement that leaps off the page to get my attention. I don't know what you're selling."

3. By the quality and design of your printed materials. With me, this is particularly important. I spend a fortune on glossy four-color brochures because I want people to know I am a seasoned professional and charge accordingly. If there are production values in what you do or deliver, the marketing materials you send out should reflect this. When communications expert Joan Minninger decided to expand her successful Civil Service seminars into training programs for major corporations, she invested more than she could afford at the time in watermarked stationery. Later she learned that her first big contract, at General Electric, was partly due to her impressive letterhead.

4. By the compatibility of the image you project with your pricing and the quality of the product or service you deliver. David Garfinkel, my co-author on the book *Guerrilla Marketing for the Imaging Industry*, tells of a retailer who saw a fabulous trade show booth for a retail-store design firm. The display must have cost more than $50,000. Yet when the retailer received the follow-up information he'd requested, it arrived on shoddy looking stationery, sloppily typed. The retailer was baffled and uneasy about the inconsistency between the impressive trade show image and the low-quality follow-through. He decided not to do business with this firm.

Your marketing image needs to communicate who you are and where you are in the market. Your marketing materials should grab attention and then convince people it's worth doing business with you. Do they?

FRIPPICISM

It's better to do something for nothing than nothing for nothing.

My friend Jeanne Robertson asked a Las Vegas cab driver, "What's the best show in town?" He quickly replied, "Oh, Jay Leno! My wife and I just went to see him. He gives a special show for taxi drivers at two in the morning. Otherwise, we could never afford to go. Kenny Rogers does the same thing when he's in town."

You wouldn't think that anyone as big in the entertainment field as Jay Leno or Kenny Rogers needs to do something for nothing, but they do. Both realize that some of the best word of mouth advertising they could have would be taxi drivers raving about their shows.

This marketing strategy extends to freelancing too. My sister-in-law, Toyah Willcox, is a West End star in England and makes good money from television commercials and television presenting. Yet she often works for next to nothing in regional productions of Shakespeare and BBC specials of other classics. Why? First, she gets to do quality creative work which is very satisfying. Second, she works with some of the top creative people in the country which is very exciting. Some of the best things you do, you don't get paid for immediately. You are making a long-term investment.

In the men's hairstyling business, I worked on commission. One of my clients, stockbroker Don Collin, suggested I phone six of his friends and tell them I wanted to style their hair. I did. Some said "no," some said "yes," and some asked if their first styling would be free. I said "yes" because I knew it's better to do something for nothing than to do nothing for nothing when you are building your business.

The key point is I was targeting customers who could afford me if they were happy with my service. Many stylists who weren't busy just sat around and read the newspaper. By offering free samples, I was practicing, my work was out walking around so others could admire it, and my prospect was likely to return as a regular customer.

One of my clients, Allen White, owned a store called The Wright Shop for Gentlemen that sold custom-made suits and expensive shoes. He became what I call a "professional friend." He presented his good customers with a gift certificate I had printed that said "To further enhance your appearance, The Wright Shop would like to present you with a gift certificate for a haircut at Miss Fripp's." I realized that if his customers could afford a custom suit and good shoes, they were also a good candidate for the services of my salon.

Is there something productive you can be doing instead of nothing? Something that is an investment in the future? How can you demonstrate or give a sample of what you're selling or presenting?

FRIPP FABLE

Young Jay Leno used to drive four hours from Boston to New York just to get five minutes on the open mike at Bud Friedman's Improv Comedy Club. "I finally put him on," says Friedman, "not because I thought he was any good then, but because he'd driven so far." Jay Leno was doing something for nothing, and eventually it paid off.

FRIPPICISM

Accept that you can't please all the people all the time.

N o one can go through life *never* making an unpopular decision, but don't slam any doors unnecessarily. People who like you or, at the very least, respect you, are more likely to do business with you or recommend you for a new position. Roger Ailes, communication coach to Presidents Reagan and Bush, wrote, "The silver bullet in business and politics is the 'like factor.' All things being equal, we are more likely to vote for people we feel we like."

But sometimes, despite all our efforts, someone isn't going to like us. *Accept it!*

We all get performance appraisals of some sort, whatever we do in life, and we have to learn how to use them and benefit from them. Even speakers like me get audience evaluations and are very sensitive to them.

Now, I know you are going to find this very hard to believe, but not all my own evaluations are raves. One of my most brilliant speeches, one which earned me top reviews, apparently pressed one woman's buttons. She sent me a card covered margin to margin with scathing verbal abuse in the tiniest script I've ever seen. She didn't sign it, but she enclosed it in a Hallmark card. A very nice touch. (Even with a hate letter, she cared enough to send the very best).

What did I learn from this experience? That it is impossible to please *all* the people *all* the time. No matter how good you are, you won't always get 100 percent approval because people have their own expectations and agendas.

Sure, negative criticism hurts and much of it is unwarranted, but be strong enough to look through the irrelevant for the tips that will improve your performance. You won't grow without such feedback. After all, everyone makes mistakes. Years ago, my brother auditioned Elton John for his band, King Crimson, and rejected him. He didn't think Elton could sing.

> ## FRIPPICISM
>
> *The "secret" of success is to love what you do for a living.*

I've always loved what I do for a living the way some people love their hobbies and recreation. People who work smarter have found a passion that goes way beyond any paycheck. You may work hard eight hours a day, but you'll rarely achieve anything exceptional in that time. Most of my working life I've worked twelve hours a day minimum, six or seven days a week, but because I love what I do, I've never felt put-upon. That doesn't mean I've loved every *aspect* of what I do, but the total picture is irresistible.

Carole Kelby has this passion. She sold $13 million worth of homes averaging $100,000 each in a lean year. From the time Carole entered the real estate business until she became a top seller, most realtors were crying the blues. Yet I know from meeting people who worked with her or who lived in her area that many of them thought she was the exclusive Realtor for this particular section of town. That wasn't true, but it was the perception. Years later, I asked her how she did it.

"Once I listed the home of a gentleman who was buying his next house directly from the builder. That meant no money for me on that part of the transaction. However, I realized that if he paid me a commission for selling his house, he wasn't going to qualify for a loan. There was only one thing I could do. 'Get out a pen,' I said. 'I'm going to tell you how to sell your present house yourself.' He was astonished and wanted to know why on earth I'd help him avoid paying me a commission. 'I guess you call it the cost of doing business,' I told him. 'You don't get paid for everything you do.'"

The man called her the next day and asked, "Do you know what I do for a living?"

"Yes," she said, "you work in personnel for a big company."

"I'm *in charge* of personnel," he told her. "We just merged with another company, and we're hiring 4,000 new people. Many of them will be relocating, and they're all yours."

Carole laughs. "At the time, I thought, what if he's lying and he only sends me a hundred?"

What investment are you making in nurturing relationships and making positive PR? There is always a payoff in the end.

FRIPP TIP

Be employable, not just employed.

No matter what you do, you need to become the Chairman of the Board of your own career. I certainly advocate being loyal to your company. It's good for your career, and it's the right thing to do. However, your goal is to be employable, *not* just employed. While you're loyal and dependable, be sure you're visible in your company, your community, and your industry. Then, if (or *when*) you are out of work, the word goes out, "Oh, good, there's a wonderful person available."

Get in Touch,

Keep in Touch

FRIPPICISM
Technology does not run an enterprise. Relationships do.

S taying in touch is as important as getting in touch. Many years ago, when top sales trainer Bill Gove was a sales manager for the 3M Company, he wrote his customers thank-you notes. One day a friend teased him, "Hey, Bill, all you do all day is write notes."

"No, just seven minutes a day," said Bill. "Everybody who does business with me hears from me at least once every three months, while my competition is calling on them, asking for their business."

Remember, there are two types of people to market to: those who know and love you and those who never heard of you. Most people spend a fortune trying to do business with people who have never heard of them, but the most important thing in sales is to stay in touch with the people who already know you.

Even when you send out cover letters attached to a brochure, make them a human bridge that connects you to the catalogue and the catalogue to the recipient so they want to read it. Help them to think, "Oh, good. This person is interested in helping me solve a problem."

Some inexpensive ways to communicate with the people who don't know you yet are:

Web sites: A sales person who works 24 hours a day and never asks for overtime. People all over the world contact me because my web site has a worldwide presence. It is also a great positioning tool. Looking at my impressive web site, you'd think I was a much larger organization than I am. I list dozens of articles that people can download free for their own education or to reprint in their professional magazines and company newsletters. I give these to people free as long as they provide contact information at the end of the article.

Journal articles: I'm a regular columnist for several publications. I then reprint these articles and put them in my press kit, again with contact information on the bottom.

List servers: Now, using a list server software program, I can send out my regular e-mail newsletters, *Frippnews* and *Speakerfrippnews*, full of business and speaking ideas. I offer useful advice and ask for nothing in return. All I want is for people to remember who I am and where they can reach me. You can do this with your own customers, saying something like, "Many of our customers tell us they get their best ideas from reading case histories of our other customers. Would you like to get a special newsletter with these success stories, tailored to large or small businesses?" Then, once a month, send out the best case history.

E-mail is terrific. (Just don't lick the stamps!) I have always run small- or medium-sized businesses. Over the years, I have done a very good job of keeping in touch with the people and companies I've worked with or who have inquired about my services. But, until a few years ago, there was no practical way I could keep in touch with the tens of thousands of audience members. *Not until e-mail!* It's an inexpensive way to keep in touch while offering something of value. It costs only your time to put a newsletter together plus a monthly fee for a list server. Keep your e-mail newsletters short, not too often, and of real value. My own e-mail newsletter carries the message: "If this does not serve you, I'll take you off the list."

Targeted Freebies: With the free gift certificates I offered through Allen White's The Wright Shop for Gentlemen, I was targeting men who could obviously afford my services since they bought custom-made suits and expensive shoes. From my stockbroker Don Collin, I received the names of six friends in his income bracket, some of whom got free stylings. None of the recipients of these "freebies" were people who wouldn't be able to afford me. Even today, as a speaker, I sometimes waive my fee for a high-profile meeting industry event full of hundreds of people who could hire me. These are all targeted freebies.

Keep in touch with your customers, prospects, and contacts. Use high-tech, low-tech, or no-tech…just as long as you're creative and effective. How many connections did you make today?

FRIPP TIP

Make Sales Meetings Work for You

Inefficient sales meetings can be one of the biggest time wasters in your business.

- Start on time. The moment people assume that meetings will start late, they'll gradually show up later and later.

- Have an agenda and a set time frame. If it's going to be a short meeting, stand up. Don't let people get too comfortable.

- Have a time limit. Schedule meetings at the end of the day or before lunch when people want to leave. It's amazing how quickly they'll get down to business.

- Explore the power of tele-conferencing and video-conferencing to save travel time. When your salespeople or downlines are in other cities, it's a great way to connect with larger groups.

FRIPPICISM

It's not who you know. It's how well you maintain your Rolodex™.

Charles was my first boss in America. I was twenty years old, working in the beauty salon of the Mark Hopkins Hotel in San Francisco. Charles was a great guy, a good hairstylist, and a lousy businessperson. He left the city for two years. Then he came back and found he had to start over from scratch. He had never kept a customer list on a Rolodex™ or in a card file.

Today we can record our customers on a computerized contact-management database system, coding each name so we can select which mailings, specials, and offers to send to each category. This way, even though we're not sending personalized letters, they are addressed individually to the recipient and sound personal because we are aware of our last contact: "You bought a book" or "You hired Patricia to speak last year."

Has any information on your business card changed in the last nine months? Have you changed companies, area codes, or your e-mail address? I ask this question when I deliver in-house training and often find 65 to 70 percent of those present have made some change. With general audiences, it runs as high as 90 percent. This proves how inaccurate your information can be.

The most valuable information you have is about your customers and prospects.

Every time you meet a new person, their information should go into your database. (I'm sure you do this!) Keep track of their changes so you can keep in touch. This is a great lesson I learned from Charles–even if it came from watching him do something wrong.

If you have a VIP list of a hundred customers, calling them every six months to update their information is a good way to keep in touch. If you have thousands, do regular mailings and note the undelivered mail that comes back. Then correct your list. If the person is no longer with the company, call and check who has taken over the job.

If you have e-mail, do regular e-mailings to your prospects' and clients' addresses and see whose message comes back to you. It's a very inexpensive way to find out if people have changed companies. Then follow through by phone as you would with a letter that comes back. Find out where your prospect has moved to and who is now in the job. You may find yourself with an additional contact.

How good is your current contact system? What steps can you take to make it better?

> ## FRIPPICISM
>
> *The real sale comes after the sale.*

Once you've made the sale, your work is only beginning. A CPA at a major convention smugly informed me during the socializing session that she didn't need to attend my workshop on how to promote yourself and your business. "I already have more than enough customers," she said.

"Come in and stay just ten minutes," I challenged her. "If it isn't what you want, then go to one of the other sessions." Two hours later, she was still there, making copious notes. Afterwards, I asked what she had been writing. She said, "You made me realize we have plenty of business, but we're not nurturing the customers we have now so we'll continue to have them in the future."

A multi-millionaire customer from my hair salon days, Manny Lozano, gave me some advice. I don't know about you, but when a multi-millionaire gives me advice, I listen. Manny said, "I don't care if you can't squeeze another customer or stylist into your salon and if you've been booked solidly for five years, you still keep promoting. You have to convince your customers and *keep* convincing them that your salon is still the best place to come to." In other words, you keep selling after the sale.

I have followed his advice all these years and became an unabashed, relentless self-promoter of my business. To do this, I use high-tech, medium-tech, low-tech, and no-tech strategies.

> **High-tech:** web sites, e-mail, e-mail newsletters, free articles, and PR pieces distributed through computer "list servers."
>
> **Medium-tech:** customer research, keeping in touch with customers through direct mail, an 800 phone number, radio and television interviews, writing regular columns and articles for various publications.
>
> **Low-tech:** press kits, flyers, media presence (being quoted as an expert), leadership in professional associations, chairing charity events and fundraising drives, handwritten notes, an ad in the Yellow Pages, belonging to and attending meetings of business organizations.
>
> **No-tech:** PR, conversations, networking, socializing, introducing yourself memorably, impressing others with your professional appearance, building word of mouth.

Here's an example of No-tech marketing with a high payoff. When I owned my hairstyling salon, I always gave my customers three of my business cards after a haircut, saying, "One for you and two for the next two people who tell you how good you look." I trained my stylists to ask their customers if they would like to book their next appointment. We wanted to keep them looking their best.

What can you do to remind your customers when it's time to consider your service or product again?

FRIPP FABLE

An attendee at one of my talks told a customer service story. "I bought a leotard to go with my child's Halloween costume. When I got home, I realized it was the wrong size before I opened the packet. The next day, I returned it for a larger size, and the clerk said, 'You don't even know what size your own kid is?' While I was in the store, I made another purchase but accidentally put the next day's date on the check. The same clerk literally threw a pen at me across the counter and said, 'Will you initial that?'"

This woman was so irate that she reported her experiences to the store's customer service department. Do you know what they said? "Oh, that must be Anthony." This is a company who advertises, "We care about our customers." Yet they know all about Anthony, and he's still working there.

I don't believe them. Do you?

FRIPPICISM

*Bring your customers to you
by putting on an event.*

People do business with people that they've met and that other people talk about. A good way to meet people and get talked about is to put on memorable events. Remember how Jay Leno and Kenny Rogers gave shows for taxi drivers? And how Jonathan Stone gave a Bike Messenger party for the other businesses in his building? My hair salon gave a popular annual Halloween party. Last year I delivered a speech wearing a custom-made Wonder Woman costume. All of these were memorable and much-talked-about events.

In the old days, movies were promoted with all-star premieres accompanied by searchlights and live broadcasts. Today, film openings are rarely spectaculars. Nevertheless, a clever event can excite word of mouth publicity. Gary Purece, a "positioning consultant," told me how he ignited interest for the 1978 film *Grease* with John Travolta and Olivia Newton-John. "One of the most obvious things to promote about the movie was the 1950s setting, the wonderful vintage music and dancing. At screenings, we put hair cream and combs in the men's rooms, big curlers in the ladies' rooms. We had dancers in the lobbies wearing 1950s costumes–poodle skirts and tee shirts with cigarette packs rolled-up in the sleeves. Customers got in the spirit and danced too. Then they went home and told their friends. That's how we sold the film."

One of the more unusual arenas in which I enjoy significant popularity is the "death-care" world. And one of the most dynamic and resourceful individuals I've ever met, Joe Dispenza, is largely responsible for the success of Forest Lawn Cemetery in Buffalo, New York.

In the summer of 1995, Joe heard me talk about using "event strategy," doing something that brings potential customers to you and builds word-of-mouth advertising. The following summer, he put my philosophy to work.

At that time, Forest Lawn was spending $120,000 a year on direct mail, radio, and print, but sales were static. Joe already knew that potential customers shared three misconceptions about Forest Lawn. First, they thought it was only for rich Protestants. Second, they thought it was in an unsafe part of town. Third, they assumed it was full, with no room for new plots. Joe wanted to dispel these inaccuracies and personally acquaint potential customers with Forest Lawn because "people do business with people they know..."

Hold on to your hats. Joe organized a series of events, offering tours of Forest Lawn every Sunday from June through August. He rented a trolley car to bring prospective customers to see and walk around Forest Lawn, and he hired actors to impersonate famous deceased occupants. The first Sunday, sixteen people showed up.

Undaunted, Joe invited a reporter from a local newspaper to cover "Summer in the Cemetery." The reporter wrote a small piece about the event. The following Sunday, more than 300 were waiting in line for the first trolley car tour. "By the end of June, I had six trolley tours with two trolley cars running on the hour," Joe says. "We also added three nature walking tours and one two-hour historical walking tour. And they kept coming!"

Potential customers saw for themselves that Forest Lawn had plenty of room for new plots, was in a beautiful part of town, and was not at all scary. The actors portrayed current "residents" from all walks of life and from varied religions, proving that burial was not limited to rich Protestants. Joe's brief sales presentation showed prospective customers that costs were not prohibitive.

Joe's twelve-week promotion was extended to twenty weeks, through October. The cost of the entire promotion–actors, extra staff for crowd control, trolley cars and sales materials–was $48,000. "Total direct pre-need sales from people on the tours who asked to buy was $80,000-plus," says Joe. There was another $20,000 in sales from people who initially said that Forest Lawn was not the most convenient to them. After taking the "love" tour, they changed their minds and wanted their loved ones there. By the end of October, 4,222 people had toured the cemetery.

It was Joe's innovative thinking that took Forest Lawn to the rarefied air of 92 percent pre-need sales. "It put this big old cemetery in the minds of the community and got the people talking and thinking about us."

Be sure to do an "After-action Analysis" after any promotion or event. Go over each area while recent experiences are fresh in your mind, and decide if you could do it bigger, better, or with more impact. The next summer, Joe's fertile mind created even more success. The tours were still free, but you needed a ticket in advance. To apply for the ticket, people filled in a questionnaire providing contact information and indicating whether a cemetery plot had already been purchased. Joe then knew his hottest prospects.

Is what you're selling any tougher than pre-need cemetery plots? Put your brain in its creative mode. Study what your competition is doing, and come up with an innovative event to reach your target markets, to demystify your product or service, to educate potential customers about your business with a fun event so people want to come, bring their friends back, and talk about it afterward.

FRIPPICISM

People learn more when they're having fun.

Whenever you have a gathering to educate and motivate your customers or your sales people, present or future, you'll win their hearts and minds faster if they have a really good time. Here are some ideas.

A Quiz Show - Before I spoke at a small meeting for *USA Today*, the organizers conducted a "quiz show." This was a great icebreaker and also served to educate their employees, using questions like: "Who writes the editorial column on page 19?" "What is our distribution in Cleveland?" Small prizes such as pens and note pads with the company logo were awarded. This got the audience laughing while learning (and had them fully warmed up when I came on). Why not create a fun quiz around your product or service, perhaps borrowing a format from a popular TV quiz show?

The Priorities Game - Another time I was speaking at Levi-Strauss. There were six tables, each with eight sales people. Each table received identical lists of typical paperwork that crosses a salesperson's desk each day. They then debated the priority for handling them. This was a great way to find out how the sales people thought and for management to teach them priorities. I was as amazed as management was at how many different opinions there were on handling the same thirteen items. You could create a similar list-sorting or problem-solving game, for example, about your products, prospects, or distribution areas.

Making your gatherings entertaining and exciting is also a big plus if you're recruiting for a direct-sales organization. When they see how much fun they can have with you, they are more likely to join.

FRIPPICISM

The currency of human contact is stories.

People often resist a sales pitch, but they cannot resist a good story. For all the information we have to absorb in our lifetimes, it's the stories that stick with us longest and influence us the most.

If you want to make a sale, tell stories about people enjoying your product, service, or opportunity. In sales presentations, avoid saying, "I think you should buy my widget because it's the best in the world." Say, "Eleanor, I want to tell you a story. I met a woman at the Chamber of Commerce last month who told me..." Then describe her situation and how she changed it by using the widget. Conclude, "She called me last week and said, 'I'm so glad I met you at the Chamber of Commerce because your widget has changed my life.'"

The most effective technique when you're selling a product or service is to have a third-party endorsement. The first thing people see on my one-sheet and web site is a quote from a top executive who says I am the most user-friendly, reliable speaker he knows, and he sleeps better at night when he hires me. Included in my shameless self-promotion are incredibly bold claims to impress my prospects and customers: "You're going to learn more"–"This is going to be the best"–"We guarantee."

How do I back this up? With third-party endorsements. (But any time you make a bold claim, be sure you can live up to it, or it will work against you). You may have all the other ingredients, but be sure to use specific praise from other people's mouths, not your own. Their stories about you carry more weight than anything you can say about yourself.

In companies where I teach customer service, occasionally an executive says, "Patricia, some of the people who work here have never stayed at a luxury hotel like the Ritz-Carlton or shopped at a service-oriented store like Nordstrom. They don't have these role models of good service, so how are you going to get the message across?"

"Easy," I say, "because, no matter where they shop, everyone is a customer and recognizes bad service when they get it." Then I tell my audience some of my funny stories about good and bad customer service, and I ask them to tell me theirs. In the stories, they recognize and empathize with the customers they will be serving. The next time they find themselves in difficult situations, they have these stories to refer to.

As you tell stories, people "make the movie" in their heads. They remember these movies and act on them long after they have forgotten the statistics. What human-interest stories can you share with your prospects and customers so they'll see themselves responding the way you'd like them to?

FRIPPICISM

What is the best of your best?
And does your customer know
about it?

My friend David Garfinkel (the copywriting genius) offered a thought-provoking suggestion on a walk we took through San Francisco's Golden Gate Park. "What," he asked, "was your greatest recent success?"

I thought for a moment. "I spoke for Meetings Professional International on how to develop a speech," I told him, "and the Program Chair, Scott Oliker, told me, 'Patricia, you garnered the highest evaluation scores in three years. One hundred percent of the audience rated you perfect for content and presentation.'"

Garfinkel asked, "What was the *best* thing of the best thing." In other words, he was asking me to go from the big picture to the most impressive detail.

"I had forty-five minutes," I told him, "to tell them how to outline a speech. During the networking before my speech, I asked twenty people what was their number one question about giving a talk. I wrote all twenty questions on the flip chart, and, not only did I show them how to outline a speech, I answered each of their twenty questions, proving that I had a great grasp of my subject matter."

David asked, "Do your customers and prospects know about this success and your ability to do this?"

Prolific though I am in my writing, he really made me think about how many *more* case histories and success stories I could turn into articles or columns–articles that would both inform the readers and teach them a powerful tool (as I hope this chapter is doing for you). Many of my friends say, "Fripp, you are absolutely shameless in your self-promotion, and happily you teach me how to do it for myself."

What a simple, powerful marketing concept the "best of my best" is, and how easy to follow through on. Every so often, ask yourself:

- What was my greatest recent success?
- What was the best of my best?
- Do my customers and prospects know about it?
- If not, how can I tell them?

So, dear reader, have I stimulated your imagination enough so you will create your own "best of the best" list? Start today and continue on a regular basis to develop stories about how you served your customers and how they were helped or their situation improved as a result. Use these same stories in your sales presentations and speeches. These same successes can be used in your sales letters, advertising, and on-line newsletter as you keep in touch with your customers and prospects.

We are all so busy we often forget to stop and analyze our successes. What would be at the top of your "best of the best" list right now? How will you let people know about it?

FRIPPICISM

If you want to do business with the affluent, go where they are.

What I enjoyed most about being in the hairstyling business (apart from getting a free college education every day by asking questions) was getting to know people I'd otherwise never meet or socialize with. It taught me to be comfortable dealing with people from all social levels.

One of my former assistants expanded on this in an imaginative way. Becky and her friend Barbara were always going to the opening of the opera or charity events that cost $300 per person. "How," I asked incredulously, "can you afford to go to all these expensive events?"

"We volunteer!" she told me. "We register people, take their money, give them name tags, or whatever the organizers want. When we've finished our job, we stay for the fun." What a great way to make a valuable contribution to different cultural and charitable events while becoming familiar with the people you hope to do business with eventually.

This is a great way to let everybody there know who you are, what you do, and that you're a generous volunteer and community booster. It doesn't cost you anything but time.

Which would you rather be doing? Prospecting at a networking event? Or watching a rerun of *Seinfeld*? Base your decision on where you want your life and your career to be in five or ten years. Think long-term. How are you going to meet the people that will be your best customers?

FRIPPICISM

Use "Magic Words."

There are "10 Magic Words" that get attention and results in your marketing. David Garfinkel, in our tape program, *Confessions of an Unashamed, Relentless Self-Promoter,* says, "These are words that get people's attention, excite them, and keep them reading."

1. "Free" - Everyone on the planet, from you to Bill Gates, likes to get something for free. Sports Genesis is a company that sells sports memorabilia. To attract buyers from major retail chains to their trade show booth, David's client offered each prospect a free engraved sports clock with a case of semi-precious stone. The clocks were shaped like footballs, golf balls, etc., and David had researched each buyer's favorite sport ahead of time. The promotion got the company an $80,000 order from the nation's largest retailer.

2. The person's name - That is everyone's favorite word. Instead of "you," use the buyer's name in each letter.

3. "Announcing" - This suggests immediacy, excitement and urgency.

4. "Introducing" - Ditto.

5. "New" - Ditto.

6. "Secrets" - People are intrigued by secrets. You have useful information that, until you put on your marketing hat, you might not realize are secrets. Focus on what you know that others don't. Let's say you run a pest control service. Restaurants are a logical customer, and most are familiar with such services. But suppose you do an ad or flyer that says, "Secrets of Keeping Your Restaurant's Kitchen Infestation Free." Of course, you'd have to tell prospects something they don't already know, but, as a specialist, you should know hundreds of things they don't.

7. "How to" - That's really two words, but they function as one. There are over 7,500 books currently in print that begin with those words. People are naturally curious about new ways to do things, especially things that will make their lives better. For example, "Learn How to Save Time on the Internet. We'll show you in less than an hour."

8. "Guaranteed" - Most businesses offer them, but if you have an unusual one, you'll get a lot of mileage out of emphasizing it in your letters and advertising. Even if it's only an industry-standard guarantee, if no one else mentions it and you do, you'll get more business. As George Zimmer of the Men's Wearhouse says, "I Guarantee It."

9. "Magic" - It's a powerful selling word that romances the imagination of your prospects. Your sale begins when they imagine all the wonderful things you could do for them. For example:

#1 - "Money-making Copywriting Course"

#2 - "*Magic* Money-making Copywriting Course"

10. "Easy" - Resistance drops automatically at that magic word. Find something–anything–easy about what you sell. What's easy about doing business with you? There must be something. Or what's easy about performing a task or achieving a result once your product or service is involved? Use your answer to begin your copy. If nothing is really easy, create "easy" steps: step one, step two, step three. Or conclude, "It's easy. Just pick up the phone and call..."

I always check my letters and promotions to be sure I've used some of the Magic Words. My Customer Service seminar is now called "*New* Customer Service: Getting, Keeping and Deserving Your Customers." Another topic is "Inside *Secrets* of a Speaking Master."

How many of the Magic Words are in your recent letters and promotional pieces? I guarantee that announcing new how-to's and secrets will do magic to your bottom line.

> ## FRIPPICISM
>
> *Expressing yourself with flair will increase the speed with which you succeed.*

Peter Butler is an excellent example of how to increase your reputation and visibility by speaking. Peter sells insurance and financial services. When he passed his fiftieth birthday, he decided to start running in Iron Man triathlons and other athletic events around the country.

He now gives lively talks at service clubs about his experiences. Peter starts by saying, "Running a marathon is like planning for your future." Then he tells colorful stories about the different events he's participated in. Finally he says, "For my last few minutes, I'm going to tell you the four things you should know about planning for your long-term future."

Notice that his speech is *not* a sales presentation–yet it actually is. The audience starts out knowing all about his business credentials because the club official who introduces him has read them from an introduction that Peter provides (This is standard procedure for all speakers). Then Peter's introductory remark relates his business (preparing for the future financially) to his topic (preparing for a marathon). His final minutes are his philosophy. He is tremendously effective, and people stand in line afterwards to get his business card.

Visibility is necessary for success in almost any business. When you can give a speech, you automatically increase your business reputation as well as your contacts and, ultimately, your sales. This happens even when you don't talk about your actual business. No civic or service club is going to ask you to entertain them with a commercial, but it's not hard to get on the club circuit if you have a lively, interesting topic in which your sales message is embedded.

Would you like to sell to fifty or more prospects at the same time? Well, step up to the lectern. Service organizations like Kiwanis, Rotary, Lion's or Optimist Clubs are always looking for a speaker to address its group for free. It's a win-win situation. They get a speaker at no charge. You have a terrific promotional tool, and, more importantly, you're perceived as an expert in your field. Does that sound like a good head start over your competition?

Speaking increases your efficiency. When you talk for fifty people at a service or civic club, you have more chance to do business with some of them eventually than if you met them one at a time, one on one, and look at the time you've saved. One part of your "unfair advantage" is your increased credibility with your audiences. Another is that they usually go away with your business card and the literature handouts you provide on a back table. There is a subtle but important difference between people taking something and your giving it to them. They are more likely to read and retain what they choose to take.

Yes, talking to a group of strangers can be intimidating, but keep focused on the positive impact the presentation will have on your business reputation and your bottom line. Don't expect to be a magnificent speaker the first time out. Think of it as the beginning of many long-term relationships.

Go on–speak out and profit from the experience.

FRIPPICISM
Master technique in order to abandon it.
ROBERT FRIPP

Unless you're talking to yourself in an empty room, everything you say is public speaking. Take advantage of every contact, from introducing yourself in social situations to addressing recruiting meetings and community organizations. Anyone who can speak clearly and eloquently impresses others as superior. If you can stand up and speak expressively and confidently–or at least stagger to your feet and say anything at all–you will be head and shoulders above your competition.

Everyone has knowledge and experience to share. When you clam up with nerves, you are not sharing with others or contributing to the decision process. Even though you don't want to be a professional speaker, there is no greater confidence booster in the world than being able to speak comfortably in front of others.

Your goal is to present the most valuable information possible to the people staring back at you. Anytime you tell people about your ideas, your sell-yourself technique can be as important as your message. Here's how to prepare for maximum impact so you can relax and connect with your audience.

Open strong. Don't waste your audience's time with trivialities. I heard a marketing expert open by telling Sales and Marketing Executives how nice it was to be there, how great the weather was, and how he loved the local restaurants. Who cares? No one came to hear him talk about weather and restaurants.

Wrong: "Ladies and gentlemen, I want to thank you for the opportunity to..."

Right: "In the next ten minutes I want to convince you that..."

Hook your audience with an intriguing idea or image. I helped Mike Powell, a senior scientist with Genentech prepare a speech for a women's organization. Since most of this audience might not know what scientists are like or what they do, I suggested he start by telling them: "Being a scientist is like doing a jigsaw puzzle–in a snowstorm–at night–when you don't have all the pieces–and you don't have the picture you are trying to create."

Be relevant. Try to give your audience the information they most want to hear. By now, you know the questions you're asked most often at cocktail receptions, parties or networking events. Well, put the answers to those questions in your speech. You might say, "The five questions I am most frequently asked about network marketing (or whatever your field is) are..." Pose each question to the audience and then answer them in a conversational manner, just like you would for a prospective customer. You may have never given a speech before, but you certainly have answered questions. If you're not sure what a particular audience might want to hear, talk to the program chair or the person who invited you beforehand.

Or consider topics like expert advice that worked, what you have learned from others, what you've learned that amazed you, sales you've fallen into, sales you almost lost, extraordinary sales, what you'd do differently now with your experience. As you plan your speech, jot down ideas as they come to you.

Use a three-part outline. If you're unsure how to organize your material, one good structure for both beginning and advanced speakers is the three-part, past-present-future format:

1. This is where I was.
2. This is where I am now.
3. This is how I got from there to here.

A friend of mine was asked to give a 25-minute speech for the local Board of Realtors because of her great success in real estate. I suggested she follow the time sequence outline and open like this: "Twelve years ago, when I went into the real estate business, I had never sold anything but Girl Scout cookies and hadn't done well with that. Last year, I sold $15 million of real estate in a slow market selling homes that averaged $150,000 each. Today, I'll tell you how I did that."

Focus on the bottom line. If you're trying to move the audience members to take action (for example, to buy from you), stress the results they will get if your idea is implemented. Don't offer backup information unless or until you are asked for it. It can interfere with the "big picture."

Be visual. People remember what they "see" in their imaginations. For a recent speech, my first words were a word picture: "Columbus, Ohio, December, zero degrees, 2,000 people trudging through the snow to hear four speakers..." Paint vivid story pictures of how things will be when your suggestion is acted on.

Have a strong closing. My scientist friend told our group of the frustrations of being a scientist and he closed by saying, "People often ask, 'Why would anyone want to be a scientist?'" He told of attending a particularly information-intensive medical conference. The final speaker of the day told the scientists, "I am a 32-year-old wife and mother of two. I have AIDS. Please work fast." The women's organization audience now understood what makes a scientist tick, and my friend got a standing ovation.

If the purpose of your speech is to persuade your audience to make a decision, you might conclude with something like, "Your next decision is not *if* but *how*. Not *if* you can afford to proceed, but *how* you can afford not to!"

•　•　•

Actor Jack Lemmon says about speaking, "Learn to speak because speaking takes the nerve of a bullfighter, the energy of a nightclub host, and the concentration of a Buddhist monk." All excellent qualities for a salesperson to develop. Are you ready to add speaking to your repertoire of unfair advantages?

FRIPP TIP

The future belongs to charismatic communicators who are technically competent. Does that describe you?

Don't look at where you are today. Decide where you want to be in five years. Understand that your customers are becoming more vigilant and your competition is constantly improving. That's why you have to get smarter every day and more multi-faceted. You have to embrace advancing technology at the same time you are improving your personal touch.

FRIPPICISM

Good marketing ends by asking for a specific action.

Image is important, but it's not the whole picture. Your marketing should be an arrow, pointing to the next step you want your prospect to take.

"If you want your own marketing to make money," says David Garfinkel, "ask each marketing effort you make to do its very best to bring in some bucks for you. Every effort is like a mini-business, a salesperson in print, on tape, on video, or on the platform. We're talking about an entrepreneurial approach."

Marketing needs to move your buyer one step closer to buying. That means, you must ask your customer to take a specific action.

David Garfinkel has a client who recently started a specialized service for mail order, infomercial, and on-line businesses who need to process large volumes of credit cards. Banks just aren't set up for this and often refuse such accounts. So David helped the client design a one-sheet mailer headline, "Just when our sales are really taking off, the bank pulled the plug on our merchant account." A mail order merchant on the West Coast described his experience, something that could happen to any company in any location. Then there were four frequently asked questions, ending with "What's the next step?" The answer was,

"Call John G. Jones at 1 (800) 000-0000. He'll be glad to talk to you personally and direct you to the right specialist in the Big Bucks Company."

You *must* end by asking for action. But what action? Do you want them to phone or write? Do you want them to ask for more information, or a sample or an estimate? Or do you want them to place an order? Some sellers never bother to think this through. If *you* don't know what you want them to do, why should *they* bother to figure it out? If *you* don't ask them to do it, why should they? It's your job to make it easy and lead them through the sales process, step by step.

What actions do your letters and marketing materials ask your prospects to take?

FRIPP TIP

The Four Essentials of Life

There are so many possibilities in your life. To take advantage of them, you need five things:

1. SOMETHING TO DO: a career, a passion, something to study, a cause to work for, a garden to dig in, a marathon to train for.

2. SOMEONE TO LOVE: your mate, parents, siblings, children, friends, pets.

3. PEOPLE TO SHARE WITH: all of your colleagues and loved ones, people with whom you have common interests and enthusiasms, and acquaintances in every walk of life.

4. PEOPLE TO CHALLENGE YOU: role models, mentors, cronies, students, apprentices, children, and especially people who sometimes disagree with you and therefore help you grow.

Make Things Happen

> ## FRIPPICISM
>
> *Ask yourself: "If the world were perfect, what would it look like?" Then expand your thinking to make it more so.*

W hatever you are about to do, ask yourself, "If the world were perfect, what would this particular thing look like or be like?" Of course, it can't be perfect, but too many times we compromise on a compromise, rather than compromising on perfection.

Choose your actions, not for how they affect today, but for where they'll get you a year or five years from now. What decisions can you make that will get you closer to the place you want to be?

- The unsuccessful are looking for pleasing experiences.

- The successful are looking for pleasing results.

Have a goal. Know *where* you are going, and the *how* will follow.

Nick Leone was a chef in Italy before he worked his way to America on a freighter. When the ship docked in Philadelphia, Nick jumped ship. Speaking no English and having little money, he first got a job on a hotel cleaning crew. Nick worked hard, routinely scrubbing the men's room fixtures with a toothbrush. The General Manager walked in and noticed the astonishing transformation. He summoned Nick and interviewed him about his goals, ambitions, and work ethic. When he learned that Nick had been a chef in his native country, he gave him a job in the kitchen. Nick soon worked his way up to head chef. He continued to work hard and save money until he was able to open his own catering business on Long Island.

Nick was doing well and could have stopped there, but he had a clear image of how things would be if they were perfect. He hired an architect to draw up plans for a beautiful banquet facility, the kind of place where people could hold large parties and gladly pay double or triple per person what Nick was currently charging. Using the sketches and his vision of a greatly expanded business, Leone persuaded some of his suppliers to advance him credit. With his cash freed up, Nick built the hall. It was so successful that he soon was able to build a second one. "He isn't just a chef, and he isn't just a manager," says his business partner, John McCormack. "He is a *creator*."

Before you make a choice or take an action, ask yourself, "How would this be if the world were perfect?" Then proceed toward perfection. Make your decisions for your tomorrows, not just your todays.

FRIPPICISM

Don't limit yourself to a quota. Be limitless.

Jim Longman, a successful life insurance salesman I met at a Dale Carnegie class, discovered his selling ability at age eight. One winter in Shenandoah, Iowa, he arrived a bit late for his Cub Scout meeting. The leader of the den was explaining that the Scouts had to sell one hundred boxes of Christmas cards. The money would go to the church charity.

Not realizing that the hundred boxes was the goal for the whole Scout troop, the boy trudged through the snow, knocking on doors every day after school, showing samples of cards, and collecting money. At the next Scout meeting, he was heartbroken to report that he had sold only ninety-eight boxes of cards. The leader stood in total disbelief–until the boy emptied the money from his pockets onto the table.

Patty Lake told me about a woman on her staff at Shell Services International. "She worked in Payroll for over twenty-five years," says Patty. "In all that time, she had never received a promotion. She had never been recognized for her contributions. She had never led a team or participated on a special project. She had not had a raise in several years. No one ever asked for her opinion or input. No one offered her training or development opportunities. No one had even bothered to find out if she enjoyed her job. And she was the lowest paid person in her job grade in the entire company.

"She had been given the lowest performance rating short of termination for many years. She didn't rock the boat. She just did her job and did not complain. Fortunately, I didn't know any of this because, when I started working at Shell, my manager agreed to let me give each employee a clean slate. I would not review past performance assessments nor listen to old gossip.

"Instead, I sat down with each staff member to find out about them and what they did. This woman, along with several others, expressed an interest in learning more about payroll and developing her skills and capabilities.

"I took her at her word and arranged for her to participate in the local American Payroll Association (APA) chapter. She took the basic payroll seminar offered by the national APA, took computer-application classes, and attended the statewide conference.

"She blossomed!

"Late this past fall, she led a project team for a customer's special needs project, a highly visible and very delicate undertaking. The outcome was phenomenal. She and her entire team were recognized and rewarded by the customer for their successful handling of the work. In addition, she is now leading end-user training on the newly implemented web-based time and attendance system. She regularly speaks out in team meetings and has many creative and useful ideas. And she is planning to sit for the CPP (Certified Payroll Professional) exam this fall and studies for it every day.

"When she got her performance review this March, she earned a significant raise and an incentive bonus. She cried and told me that all she had ever needed was someone to believe in her. I did and I do."

What self-limiting idea or barrier are you ready to discard? What self-limiting habits can you help others get rid of? Where can you find supportive, encouraging people?

FRIPP TIP

Coping

There are three main strategies for dealing with the multiple demands of today – personal, career, home, community.

1. **Limiting.** Avoiding conflicts by focusing totally on one area, usually career. (Efficient, but can be restrictive).

2. **Staggering.** Devoting time blocks alternately to different demands: "This year I'll concentrate on making Sales Manager, next year I'll get my body in shape, the year after that I'll go back to school and maybe get married." (May work if only one area is a priority).

3. **Juggling.** Participating in all-important areas at once, juggling the time and energy demands on an as-needed basis. (This is the hardest, and jugglers need strong support systems, both within their families and in the community).

How you choose to cope is a matter of personal style, personal resources, and what you are up against. But remember Auntie Mame's famous observation: "Life is a banquet and most poor suckers are starving!"

FRIPPICISM

If you focus on what might have been, it gets in the way of what can be.

"How many of you have had things go wrong in your business that seemed devastating at the time?" I asked an audience of entrepreneurs in San Francisco. Everyone raised a hand. Some people put up two hands.

Like people I've met, I have had a wonderful business, great employees, and many successes. I have also been disappointed, had hard-earned funds embezzled, and had people quit at the most inopportune moments. I managed to live through every single experience and grow from it.

It's relatively easy to look back at business disappointments and realize that they were just part of a regular up and down cycle. When you survive a few such cycles, you become a lot more valuable to your customers. Personal disasters are also part of the inevitable cycle called life. That's why the more we experience, the more philosophical we become about events, both business and personal, that would have been shattering when we were younger.

Larry Wilson, co-author of *The One-Minute Salesperson*, believes that most business traumas will turn out to be merely inconveniences or even springboards to something better, as soon as we can see them in perspective. I serve my audience better, not because of any success I've had, but because of my ability to adapt.

Adversity in business can be a springboard for creative thinking and new growth. One man, for example, found himself with a warehouse full of canned white salmon. Consumers, accustomed to the pink kind, wouldn't touch it until he had new labels printed: "Snow-white Alaskan Salmon-guaranteed not to turn pink in the can."

Great thinkers and creative people throughout history have thrived in periods when their work had some sort of restriction put on it, political, financial, or cultural. The symphony and the sonnet are very rigid forms, yet we have an abundance of great symphonies and sonnets. Great works have been produced in hard times, in the midst of hunger, calamity, and oppression.

When you're faced with a setback, remember:

- Any great loss involves loss of part of yourself, so realize it will take time to heal and rebuild.

- Loss can force you to redefine your priorities and goals, to refocus, and to renew.

- You *can* rebuild.

If you've tried building a sales organization or a sales career in the past and didn't achieve your goals, that doesn't mean you can't try again and succeed. You have more information now, more experience, and more determination. Don't look back at what was or might have been. Look ahead.

FRIPPICISM

Resist emotional blackmail.

A woman at a direct sales company I spoke to asked what she should do when she's going to work and her two-year-old says, "Mommy, I hate you because you're leaving." I turned to the audience for answers. One woman stood up and said, "You are allowing yourself to be emotionally blackmailed." Another woman said, "I get the same thing, and I smile and hug her and say, 'I'm going to miss you too, honey. I'll be back as soon as I can.' It's up to you whether you interpret your child's fears as blackmail or not."

Another woman came up to me at the break because she did not want to share her thoughts with the group. She said, "If I can make my mentally retarded two-year-old daughter understand that mommy is going out to make money to help buy her 'pretties,' I think somebody should certainly be able to make a normal child understand."

Blackmail is a contract between two people. It only works when both agree to play. We should not accept emotional blackmail from others, just as we should not try to blackmail them. Often society provides women with only a vague line between good manners and being taken advantage of; between being a caring, nurturing person and being a victim. It's up to the woman to make the line clear and strong, both for herself and for others. A woman named Joann told me that she used to be married to a man who treated her shabbily. Then one day she thought to herself: "If I were being treated this way by a man courting me, I wouldn't dream of marrying him." In a matter of days, she had filed for divorce and has never regretted that decision.

To teach people how we want to be treated, we must sometimes use a little muscle and refuse to be intimidated. We need to know that we deserve good treatment. If we don't respect ourselves, who will? What particular blackmail are you going to challenge?

FRIPPICISM

Clean out the closets of your life.

People who succeed in sales have more resilience than almost anyone else on earth. Mountain climbers, astronauts, and salespeople. You can't top them for endurance!

To keep yourself at maximum fitness, surround yourself with people who encourage you. Discard anyone who keeps telling you all the reasons you are going to fail.

Go over the closets of your life with the same vigilance you clean your actual closets. Periodically you go through your closets with a critical eye, weeding out the bargain shoes in the wrong color, the expensive suit you got on sale that never fit, the "great" shirt that was a gift from someone you love.

Once I had all of those fashion items in my closet. Then a wardrobe consultant friend came over and made me clean out what didn't fit or no longer represented my self-image. It was an exhilarating feeling. Now the clothes I wear make me feel and look great, and project the image I like. I also realized that my life needed the same periodic examination.

We all have a self-image closet too. Take a serious look at what you find there and clean it out. Throw out ideas that no longer fit your lifestyle or your experiences. Clean your closet of certain old friends as well–the ones who have become acquaintances. Too often we spend our energies with people whose interests have grown apart from ours. Clean out the negative people, the folks who cannot accept your achievements, insisting it's only a "fluke" when you finally attain a great goal. Their own insecurities require them to shoot other people down. It is time to let them know you are proud of your achievements, and then move on to those who will support you in your endeavors.

Closets are where we store the things we use in our daily lives. Don't let them get cluttered with outmoded clothes, unproductive ideas, and negative relationships. Clean them out!

FRIPP TIP

Some people feel that planning requires rigid scheduling with no room for experiments, side trips, or pleasure. In *Make Your Mind Work For You*, Joan Minninger and Eleanor Dugan compare nonplanners to jellyfish, "drifting back and forth between existence in the water and extinction on the shore. Farther out in the ocean are the whales and dolphins, cavorting, playing, enjoying themselves immensely, but always following their migration patterns, their plans. Is the life-plan of a whale really more restrictive than the drifting of a jellyfish?"

FRIPPICISM

Small additional increments are transformational.

ROBERT FRIPP

Good habits lead to sales success. Think big. Start small. Our habits are part of us, built up like the layers of a pearl from our own juices. They can either provide a lustrous shield against adversity–or a prison of our own making. What new habits do you want to acquire? What old habits do you want to change?

Ken Blanchard, co-author of *The One-Minute Manager*, says, "People who want to develop new habits should notice how they describe their goal. Do they say they are interested in or *commited to* this goal?"

If you are interested in your health, then you go to the gym when the weather is nice and your friends are willing to go. But if you have a commitment, you go whether you feel like it or not, no matter how late you got in the night before, and whether your pals are going with you or not. If you're committed to building a sales organization, you need the discipline of being on the phone so many hours a day, whether you feel like it or not.

Do you have an "interest in" or a "commitment to" achieving your goals and developing good work habits?

You have a choice. You can improve by experimenting with new ideas. Or you can continue doing comfortable things that don't work. If you choose the former, here is what it requires.

1. Make up your mind. Be committed to making the change. For instance, you decide to be on time rather than constantly offering excuses about what caused you to be late. You analyze the actual reasons for repeated lateness and take specific actions: getting up and/or leaving the house at a different time; changing your route or means of transportation; taking an earlier train; preparing the night before by laying out clothes, packing lunches, etc.; negotiating an end to delaying tactics of spouse or children.

2. Describe your new behavior in writing. Not only does this give you a record of what you're doing, but the physical act of writing something down and then reading it back forms the first neurochemical thread of axons in your brain that will eventually form the permanent mental chain called habit.

3. Share it. Announce the change publicly. Tell the world or at least someone in your support system. Changing habits is never easy, and you need all the boosters you can get. (Avoid the "friend" who says, "Aw, come on, cheat a little." If you run across someone this insensitive, reply in an indignant voice, "Why should I cheat myself?").

4. Act immediately–or as soon as possible. If you decide you will stop complaining, start not complaining *today*, not tomorrow. Or when you go home at the end of the day, resist the temptation to complain to your spouse, roommate, or children. Act immediately on whatever you have decided.

5. Don't give up for three weeks. That's how long it takes to form a new habit. Invest the time to ingrain your new habit. Another reason for the three-week timetable is it's a lot easier to try something different and uncomfortable when you can see an end to it, a definite time limit rather than a dreary chore stretching on forever. The "carrot" of completing those twenty-one days keeps you going. At the end of that time, either your new regime has become a habit, or its benefits are so overwhelming that you will be eager to continue it until it does become a habit.

Habits are like railroad tracks. You lay them down with a lot of effort so that later you can get where you want to be smoothly and easily. Where do you want to be? What habits will get you there?

<table>
<tr><td align="center">FRIPPICISM</td></tr>
<tr><td align="center">Learn to say "no" by saying "yes."</td></tr>
</table>

In sales, your time is as valuable as your contacts. Have you ever said "yes" when you really wanted to say "no?" Nothing eats up your time faster. It may have seemed the most efficient or popular or expedient thing to do at the moment, but you regretted it afterward.

First of all, realize you don't need to make any excuses for refusing a business proposal or social invitation. "No, thank you for asking, but I already have plans." What you don't have to explain is that your plans are with yourself. You don't have to make excuses about what you are doing. Often we think we should explain our reasons for our behavior to others as if we are responsible to them for our actions.

And fortunately there's a way to say "no" and "yes" at the same time: Refuse the request, but offer an alternative that works better for you and benefits the petitioner as well.

It has always been part of my overall marketing strategy to be well known in my community and business contacts and worthy causes often ask me to volunteer my time. Here's an example of how I handle it. An organization asked me to run a luncheon once a month for their volunteers. I said, "No. Because of my travel schedule, I won't be there often enough. However, let me tell you what I CAN do. Once a year I'll give a free talk to rev up your volunteers. That way you use a talent of mine that most of your other members don't have." I was saying "yes" and "no" at the same time: "no" to the original request, but "yes" to supporting the organization.

Debbi Steele, when she was a Sales Manager for several small hotels, told me how she handled the frequent requests to "have lunch so I can learn what it is like to be in hotel sales." She said "no" to one young woman's invitation, but gave her two choices. Either they could talk while jogging at 6:30 a.m., or the young woman could spend the afternoon in Debbi's office, stuffing envelopes and doing odd jobs while she observed Debbi handling the phones. They would talk while they worked. The young woman chose option two, and later thanked my friend profusely. Both women were winners, and my friend didn't have to work late to catch up after an extended lunch.

Often I receive thirty to forty calls a month from people who want to take me to lunch so they can ask me questions about the speaking industry. I reply, "No, I can't have lunch with you, but I'll give you five minutes right now. If we were at lunch, what would you ask me?" Most can't think of a question! And if they can, the questions are often so naive that I can refer them to an article on my web site (Any time people keep asking you the same question, automate the answer! Recently I telephoned a hotel from the airport and asked for driving directions. I was transferred to a recording with the options to repeat the message and to return to a live operator. That's true service, but look how much staff-time the hotel saved).

Before you say "Yes," ask yourself:

- Do I really want to do what I've been asked to do?

- Will I benefit personally from the experience?

- Will those closest to me benefit?

- Will I ever have the opportunity to do this again?

- How much of my time is involved?

- Can the job be done quickly or will it involve weeks, months, or even years?

- How much help will I have, or do I have full responsibility?

- Am I being asked to do this job because I'm right for it or because I usually don't say "No"?

- Will my family or friends have to take a back seat while I'm involved?

- Will I have to cancel other plans in order to make this new commitment?

If you don't have the right answers to these questions, teach yourself to say, "No, thank you, I already have plans." Or to say "yes" by saying "no."

FRIPPICISM

Save fifteen minutes a day, and you'll gain two extra weeks a year.

How do you find the time to achieve everything you want to achieve? Suppose you were suddenly given the gift of two extra weeks each year to do anything you wanted. How would you spend this time? What would you want to accomplish? Would you increase your efforts on an existing project? Start something new? Or even use it as restorative personal time?

This gift is not a fantasy. Eliminating just fifteen wasted minutes each day adds up to ninety-one extra hours a year, more than two full work weeks. Here are some simple ways to achieve this "miracle."

1. Separate efficiency and effectiveness. Don't confuse activity with accomplishment. Management expert Peter Drucker defines them like this:

- Efficiency is doing things right.

- Effectiveness is doing the right things.

There is no point doing well what you shouldn't be doing at all. First, make the hard decisions about what you want and need to do. Then do them, and do them right (You've probably heard someone say, "I don't have time to get organized," or even "I don't have time to do it correctly right now, but I'll come back later and fix it"–as if the future holds limitless time to undo and redo something done poorly.)

2. Underbook. Your calendar is probably full as you try to squeeze in everything you need and hope to do. As hard as it may seem, don't overbook. Don't list an activity in every single space during every waking hour. Instead, be realistic! Write in time buffers, and plan for unexpected emergencies. They'll take less time to resolve, and you'll stay cool and positive if you know you've allowed for them. Underbooking will actually allow you to achieve more.

3. Block-book for big projects. Some projects can't be picked up and put down easily. Block-book your high priority items. Schedule at least one uninterrupted hour a day. Early in the morning is good if you're a morning person–at home before the family gets up or at the office before anyone else arrives–but some people prefer lunchtime at the office, before dinner, or late at night after everyone is in bed.

4. Multitask. Combining or piggybacking tasks makes you more efficient.

- While you're holding on the phone, sign letters or checks or mark magazine articles you want to read later.

- In small buildings, don't wait for elevators–take the stairs. It's good exercise, and you'll get there sooner.

- Have a meditation break instead of a coffee break.

- Listen to motivational tapes (mine if you like!) while commuting or traveling.

- When you plan to meet someone, do it in a place where you can accomplish something while you're waiting.

5. Confirm. Save yourself hours of wasted time by confirming ALL appointments and flights. Yes, it takes time to confirm, but the payback can be enormous.

6. Do it now. One of the biggest time wasters is waiting to do something until it doesn't matter any more. You lose more than just time. You surrender control to others or to random chance. And you sacrifice your two-week time bonus.

Some things have to be done perfectly. Some don't. Don't strive for perfection in items or actions that don't matter. People are usually paid to get results, not to be perfect.

Indecision is one form of procrastination. There is a time for deliberation and a time for action. The well-known prayer might be altered to "Lord, give me the patience to wait for the right moment, the energy to act decisively, and the wisdom to know when to do which."

Decide. Do it. And don't waste your time on regrets or rehashing decisions, justifying bad ones, or salvaging poor time investments that ought to be written off. Use the past as a guide for the future, not as an excuse for not dealing with it.

There! You've just saved yourself weeks of time. What will you do with it?

FRIPPICISM

Learn to be smarter today than you were yesterday.

Someday I'm going to write my own version of Robert Fulghum's bestseller, *All I Really Need to Know, I Learned in Kindergarten*. Only mine will share the simple lessons I learned standing behind a hairstyling chair, lessons that can apply to any business.

For example, my first job at age fifteen was in a glamorous hair salon in England. As soon as I'd get to know my rich women clients, I'd always ask them specific questions: "What were you doing when you were my age? How did you make your money? Did you make it yourself or did you marry it? If you made it yourself, how did you do it? If you married it, where did you meet him?" All this was good "market research."

Later, I was one of the first women to go into men's hairstyling. That was back in 1969, when the neighborhood barbershop was a social institution, a place where men gathered to hang out, chat about sports, and even get "a little off the sides and back." All haircuts looked roughly alike. Men's hairstyling represented a major sociological shift.

My customers were executives from the San Francisco business community, men who wanted to look distinctive, who socialized in the boardroom, and who had no time for browsing through back issues of *Field and Stream*. Sometimes we would do someone's hair and see him in the Wall Street Journal the next week. It was a fabulous learning opportunity for me, and my questions now centered on the business world: "What makes you the best salesperson in your company?" "What's the biggest challenge in your business?" "How did you turn your little company into a million dollar enterprise?" Their answers made me smarter about a wide variety of industries.

This was in the days when "small talk" between stylist and customer was the rule. One day I confronted my staff. "You are all bright, interesting people," I told them. "Why do you talk such a load of drivel, when the most fascinating minds are sitting in your chairs? You are missing out on a fantastic opportunity!"

The best thing about my current career as a speaker is that I'm still getting paid to learn about a lot of businesses and occupations. Even though my audience may work in a particular sector, I can share new and different information with them from other industries, information that can have a profound impact on their thinking.

Isn't that one of the big advantages of meeting a lot of different people in your own business? The more you learn what works for them and the more you retain this information, the smarter you get and the more expert you become in advising your customers.

I'm a great believer that if we are going to be exceptional, *every single day* has to be a learning experience. The best way to do this is to ask questions. Question the people you're doing business with; question the people you *hope* to do business with; question your friends who are successful in other industries and see how you could apply their techniques to your own career. Get smarter every day.

FRIPP TIP

Like it or not, we are the only ones in charge of our actions and reactions. It may be very comforting to see others as the manipulators of our behavior and the source of all our woes, but it is a real time waster. The day that you discover that you are in charge of you is the day you turn your life around.

The type of person you are is the type of world you live in. Your perception of the world is your reality. To turn a popular expression around, "What you get is what you see."

Our perceptions of the world become our world. They can brighten the dark corners or cast impenetrable gloom over the most luminous parts. The message is clear, isn't it? No matter what you do, no matter what happens to you, be responsible for yourself. Stop making excuses! Stand on your own two feet. Believe you can do it.

FRIPPICISM

If you can change your thinking just a few degrees, you'll see a whole new world.

Often, in sales, we get discouraged. The next time you do, remember this story. One Sunday morning, I was running in the Marina District of San Francisco with a psychiatrist friend of mine, David Leof. We jogged along the bay from the Marina Green to the Golden Gate Bridge and back again.

Afterward, we were walking to cool down. The sky was clear and full of seagulls, the water was blue and full of boats, and the bridge arched over the entrance to the harbor. As we turned back toward our car, the picture changed completely, now a vista of greenery, kites, joggers stretching, and rows of neat Spanish-style houses.

David said, "You see what we've just done, Patricia? We have just turned around a few degrees, and it's like we're looking at two totally different pictures. The good thing about my practice is that people only have to change their thinking a few degrees to have totally different lives."

We've all heard people say, "Well, it's not working where I am. I think I'm going to move to another state, go into a different line of business, lose fifty pounds, or bleach my hair blonde, and then my life will work." When it comes to good mental health, sometimes what we really need to do is realize what we already have to be grateful for. Just change your thinking a few degrees. The next time you feel stale or frustrated, look at where you are and what you have from a slightly different angle.

Very often salespeople get discouraged. After a day of "nos," remember David's advice. Start the next day fresh by changing your thinking a few degrees. Stop for just thirty seconds and focus on the last time you made a sale, you felt appreciated, or any other great success. This can be more inspiring than a week's vacation! You're now armed to face the world and its new opportunities.

Go out and make it so you don't have to fake it!